SOUND RETIREMENT PLANNING

REVISED AND UPDATED

A RETIREMENT PLANNING JOURNEY DESIGNED TO
ACHIEVE: CLARITY, CONFIDENCE & FREEDOM

JASON R. PARKER

Sound Retirement Planning
A retirement planning journey designed to achieve clarity, confidence and freedom
Copyright © 2018 by Jason R. Parker.

Address all inquiries to:
Jason R. Parker
9057 Washington Ave NW #104, Silverdale, WA 98383
360-337-2701 | info@parker-financial.net
www.parker-financial.net
www.soundretirementplanning.com

Published by:
Jason R. Parker

ISBN-13: 978-1-727-74986-1
ISBN-10: 1727749863

Editor: Tyler Tichelaar:
Back Cover Photo: Gary Bowlby Photography
Interior Book Design: Fusion Creative Works
Interior Illustration: Rebecca Lynn Parker

Every attempt has been made to properly source all quotations.

Printed in the United States of America

Second Edition

DISCLAIMER AND LIMIT OF LIABILITY

DEDICATION

TO REBECCA, MY BEAUTIFUL WIFE AND BEST FRIEND:

Thank you for your love, kindness, and encouragement.
I am inspired by the life you lead.

TO OLIVER AND LIBBY, MY AWESOME CHILDREN:

The most important title I have ever had is dad.
I hope I can live up to it.

ACKNOWLEDGMENTS

Much of the success I have experienced wouldn't have been possible if it weren't for some very important people.

First, I have the greatest family a man could ever ask for. My wife, Rebecca, is my inspiration and encouragement. Without her I wouldn't have the great life I have today. She keeps me focused on what's truly most important in my life, which is my faith, family, and the relationships we create along the way. We have two beautiful, healthy, and vibrant children, and it's my greatest honor to hold the title of dad.

Dean Schennum was my mentor. He had more than thirty years of experience in the financial services arena, and Parker Financial never would have become what it is today without his guidance, support, insight, and sense of humor.

Heather Henrichsen is my chief operations officer. Heather is brilliant, super-efficient, and a great asset to our firm. Because of Heather's editing and journalism experience, this book is ten times better than it would have been.

No man is an island. I'd like to say that I created and engineered every system or concept you will read about in these pages. Unfortunately, that isn't the case. I surround myself with some of the top advisers in the country, and I am dedicated to always learning. My company would not be where it is today if it weren't for the opportunity to tap into the insight and experience of some of the greatest advisers in the country and, for that, I am grateful.

PREFACE

In 2014, the first edition of *Sound Retirement Planning* was published. What an honor to see my book make it to the #1 best seller in personal finance on Amazon and hold that position for a few weeks. Having a book that became a best seller has created many opportunities, and I've enjoyed being a guest on ABC, NBC & FOX television stations. My mother-in-law likes to tease me about being a celebrity because she remembers the early days when I had long hair and a goofy-looking beard when I first started dating her daughter, Rebecca, my wife of 21 years.

Thank you to everyone who has purchased my book and recommended it to your friends. In 2009, I began hosting a radio show in the Seattle area called *Sound Retirement Radio*. The show is still going strong, and you can now download each episode as a podcast on itunes.

I have a unique perspective in the retirement planning community. On one hand, I get to interview some of the great minds in finance to understand their perspectives on the economy, investments, insurance and retirement planning. But unlike some, who only work as financial journalists, I have also had the opportunity as an adviser and the president of a wealth management firm to work with hundreds of real people and help them on their journey into and through retirement. So I get to learn from the industry experts, but I also get to work with real people and hear about their dreams and fears as they make this transition. I've had the good fortune to help plan 50th wedding anniversary family vacations, celebrate the birth of grandchildren and help them the plan for college savings. I've walked life with people who have been diagnosed with dementia, sat at the bedside of people dying and attended my fair share of memorials and celebrations of life. My book is a collection of what I've learned from the people we serve about living a good life and the financial planning to support a great retirement.

A lot has changed in the financial world since 2014. New leadership is changing health insurance options. In the new and updated version of my book I now have a chapter on health insurance considerations both before age 65 and after age 65, when most people enroll in Medicare.

In 2017 we developed and launched software called *Retirement Budget Calculator* to help people who are preparing for retirement develop a better spending plan. As I write this, the economy is strong and unemployment is low. But at the same time, the stock market is trading at some of the highest valuations seen in recent history and interest rates have started to increase, which is putting pressure on bonds and assets related to interest-rate risks.

I'm committed to learning, teaching and sharing what I have learned from the amazing people we get to serve. I hope you find the new edition of *Sound Retirement Planning* better than ever. Now more than ever people are looking for sound financial advice so they can feel confident they will be able to achieve their lifestyle goals in retirement.

To help with this ever-changing retirement landscape, I realized I needed to update my book. As I began updating the book, I realized this was more than just an update since I was adding a lot of new ideas and information. I changed the order of the chapters so the flow of the new book more closely matches the actual planning process we personally use for coaching hundreds of real people as they prepare for and transition through retirement.

This book has been completely updated, significantly improved. Much of the same information from my first book is included, but *Sound Retirement Planning* is better than ever. I hope you'll agree.

Radio and podcast guests do not endorse nor recommend any of the views nor opinions expressed by Jason Parker. Nor does Jason Parker or Parker Financial LLC endorse or recommend any of the views or opinions expressed by radio or podcast guests. All company names, brand names, trademarks and logos are the property of their respective owners.

THIS BOOK INCLUDES POWERFUL YET SIMPLE AND EASY-TO-UNDERSTAND CONCEPTS ON:

- Lifestyle design — focusing on what is most important in retirement

- Tips for how to maximize your Social Security income

- How to diversify your money to make sure it lasts as long as you do

- Estate planning and the legal documents you should consider

- Tax planning tips for retirement

- Understanding inflation and how to fight back

- Protecting your family from an unforeseen health care event

- How to maximize your cash flow and income in retirement

- Forward-looking approaches to asset allocation and diversification in this new economy

- Strategies for reducing the fees you pay

- Health insurance options when planning retirement

As you read through these pages my hope is the work I am doing will add significant, meaningful value to your life. If this book makes an impact on you, then I'd like to connect with you on Facebook and hear more about your story. Join our community at www.facebook.com/SoundRetirementPlanning where we teach you ways to plan for your retirement to help you achieve clarity, confidence and freedom in your retirement years.

WHAT IS A SOUND RETIREMENT PLAN?

Imagine you just retired. You visit your mailbox to find year end statements and tax related documents for multiple accounts. You now realize that over a lifetime of saving and investing, you have multiple accounts at various financial institutions. At the time, making those investments made perfect sense, and there was a reason for each investment decision. But now, as you look at this hodgepodge of statements, you might realize that these accounts are not working together to support your retirement goals. When you visit a financial adviser, you learn that while you were purchasing different mutual funds, many of those funds were investing in the same companies. So while you thought you were diversified, you now realize you actually have a lot of overlap and highly correlated investments.

Now that you are retired you understand that your most valuable asset is your time. You become more aware of the amount of time you spend opening statements, collecting tax documents, reading prospectuses, dealing with corporate actions, logging into various custodians, preparing your taxes and trying to keep track of it all.

This reality drives many people we serve to take action to consolidate, optimize and simplify their financial lives.

Consolidation is the first step in unifying your financial life. You start by putting all of your eggs under one umbrella, but at the same time remaining diversified by having all those eggs in different baskets under the one umbrella.

Optimization is when you create a diversified strategy that will best support your lifestyle in retirement. The focus of diversification in retirement should be on cash flow. An optimized and efficient retirement income strategy should keep your fees as low as possible, reduce unnecessary taxation and be coordinated with your retirement cash flow plan.

Simplify means your retirement plan should be easy to understand, and you should be able to explain it to a 7 year old. Albert Einstein once said, "I am not a genius. I am just curious. I ask many questions, and when the answer is simple, then God is answering."

Henry David Thoreau said, "Our life is frittered away by detail. Simplify, simplify."

Retirement does not have to be complicated. I encourage you to consolidate, optimize and simplify your financial life as you prepare for retirement.

ALL OR NOTHING

One of the challenges many people have when creating a retirement income plan is they meet with ten different financial advisers, and end up with ten different opinions about the right way to create a plan.

Most of the disagreement among financial advisers will be based on which financial vehicles you should use to implement your plan. Investment advisers tend to recommend stocks, bonds, mutual funds and ETFs. Brokers tend to recommend commission-based mutual funds, variable annuity contracts and alternatives such as REITs and limited partnerships. Insurance agents tend to believe strongly in the use of fixed annuities and life insurance contracts.

There really is no magic bullet, no perfect financial vehicle. Creating a retirement income plan does not have to be an all or nothing decision. Combining the use of these different financial vehicles to create a plan is often a better solution than being committed to only one way of thinking or the use of one financial vehicle.

Understand that all of the different financial vehicles that exist today are better at some things than others. They all have some sort of fee associated with them and someone is making money as a result of the path you choose. My recommendation is to keep an open mind. Look at the advantages and disadvantages of the different financial vehicles that are being recommended and make sure that they are being recommended as part of a comprehensive plan and not just a product being sold to you.

As you read through the chapters, it may seem at times that I am repeating ideas. And that's because I am. There is an old saying that "repetition is the mother of all learning." If I repeat it, then it's because it is important.

CONTENTS

Introduction

CORE CONCEPTS

I often say I work with some of the greatest people in the country. These people whom I serve daily have blessed me with their wisdom.

Below are some quotes and core concepts they've introduced me to that have shaped my life, this book, and my firm. I firmly believe that this practical wisdom helps my clients plan for their retirement in ways that help them achieve clarity, confidence and greater financial freedom.

- *The rich rule over the poor, and the borrower is slave to the lender.* — Proverbs 22:7

- *An investment in knowledge pays the best interest.* — Benjamin Franklin

- *It's not about how much you make; it's about how much you keep.* — Author Unknown

- Retirement is all about cash flow, not net worth.

- Pay your fair share of taxes, but not a penny more.

- *I'm more concerned with the return of my money than the return on my money.* — Will Rogers

- Cash is king, aka the Golden Rule: "He who has the gold makes the rules."

- *Begin with the end in mind.* — Stephen Covey

- Don't confuse tax preparation with tax planning. Tax preparers are looking back, making sure the right numbers are in the right boxes. Tax planning is looking forward for ways to reduce your future tax liability.

- Don't put all your eggs in one basket. Diversify your time horizon as well as your investments.

- Seek independent, non-biased counsel that exercises fiduciary responsibility.

- Time is the cure to volatility in the stock market. Make sure time is on your side.

- Keep your fees low.

- One momma can take care of eight babies, but eight babies can't take care of one momma.

- Make your legacy about quality time spent with loved ones, not the money you leave behind.

- *Insanity: Doing the same thing over and over again and expecting different results.* — Albert Einstein

- Make Jesus the Lord and Savior of your life and put God first.

WHY YOU NEED THIS BOOK

The world has changed dramatically in the last couple of years. Our government is printing money at an unbelievable pace. Ten thousand baby boomers are retiring every day. Taxes are at historical all-time lows and, in my opinion, are likely to go up. Our national debt is growing exponentially every year. Our government has recently bailed out financial institutions, taken over private companies, and has voted for one of the largest overhauls to our healthcare system in our country's history. The stock market's volatility is high, and what once appeared to be sage advice has turned into questionable theory. In fact, some people have recently said that "buy and hold" in the new economy should now be titled "buy, hold, and hope."

But more important than any of these external factors is making sure you have money for your retirement. If you are reading this book, then you are probably either just about to retire or already retired. While I certainly don't expect to fix all of the country's problems with this book, I will give you a plan for getting the very most out of your retirement and helping you take action to achieve your retirement lifestyle goals with a high degree of confidence.

As the president of a wealth management firm that specializes in retirement, I have had the opportunity to meet with hundreds of people and help them on this very important journey into and through retirement. When I meet with people, they generally share the same five primary concerns:

- They never want to become a burden to their family either physically or financially.

- They don't want to run out of money before they run out of retirement.

- They want to pay in a legal manner as little in taxes as possible.

- They want to earn a fair rate of return on their money and outpace inflation with the least amount of volatility in their retirement portfolio.

- This last concern is probably the biggest one of all: They fear making an irreversible mistake.

Many of the people I meet tell me, "What I have is what I have." Now that they are no longer employed and not contributing to their retirement accounts, they feel concerned and restless about their investment decisions. Many prospective clients told me they experienced a 30-60 percent decline in their investment values in 2008, and they don't want that type of volatility now that they are retired. *When did it become okay for retired people to be in situations where they could lose 50 percent of everything they have invested in one year?*

If you share in any of these concerns, then I'd encourage you to buy this book. At my wealth management firm, we are very specialized in the work we do, and because we are always researching academic and industry solutions to many of these issues, I want to share with you what I have learned through both my research and real-life experience.

Theory and practical application are two very different animals. A financial journalist talks about ideas that might work, but an adviser has worked with real people and real money to help them achieve their retirement goals. If financial journalists make mistakes, they can always retract or rewrite their opinions. But if retirement financial advisers make a mistake, the people they serve deal with devastating real-world consequences.

Being a financial adviser is a tremendous responsibility, and often people's financial welfare lies on the adviser's shoulders. That you are looking for sound financial advice is probably one reason you are reading this book. As an adviser who operates in a fiduciary capacity with the goal of always acting in my clients' best interests, I want to make sure I am doing my due diligence to ensure my clients are experiencing the desired outcome. I am more conservative than the average journalist or academic theorist because I have a lot more on the line than just selling a few books.

An old saying exists among the gardeners of life, "You want to be green and growing, not brown and wilting." To me, this philosophy means you must always be growing, learning, and challenging yourself because if you ever stop, you will wilt and die. I have the best intentions based on the best planning that I have discovered during my years in practice. I don't know of any better planning, but what works today may not be the best tomorrow. I am committed always to learning, discerning, and implementing what I believe are the best ideas available.

WHAT THIS BOOK IS NOT

A few years back, the furnace in my home broke, and I called a repairman to fix it. He was probably in his mid-sixties and very confident in his occupation. He popped the cover off the furnace and within twenty minutes had completely pulled my furnace apart, cleaned a few things, replaced a few pieces, and Shazam! He was done.

He handed me a bill for about $200 dollars. Talk about an hourly wage! Being the curious guy I am, I asked him what had been wrong with my furnace. He spent the next fifteen minutes talking to me in technical terms. He could have been speaking Japanese since it would have had the same impact on me. I just stood there nodding my head and wondering, "What in the world is this guy talking about?"

Now this gentleman was an expert, and he had probably forgotten more about my furnace than I will ever learn. That's exactly the kind of person I want to fix my furnace. I don't want to become a furnace repair expert, so I am willing to pay for his expertise. But at the same time, I realized he was assuming my level of knowledge was on par with his.

Unfortunately, I realize that many financial advisers assume the people they serve have the same level of comprehension on financial matters that they do. I spend up to ten hours a day working in my industry and learning the ins and outs of investing and all of the terminology that comes with it. But I can't expect my clients to have time to do the same. Therefore, this book is not a textbook for financial professionals. I am not trying to write a course for those who, like me, spend all of their days studying this industry.

This book is intended to share ideas, concepts, and strategies in a language that is relevant and accessible to the average person. While I will discuss some of the benefits of the work that financial advisers do, I won't spend a lot of time talking about the disadvantages. With any investment or insurance product, you need to understand all of the advantages and disadvantages before making a decision, and you should consult with a qualified adviser who can help you make sense of these ideas and lead you to understanding which ones may be best for your situation.

Every financial decision has positives and negatives. When it comes to your investments, you always get to choose from two of three possibilities:

- Rate of return

- Principal Preservation

- Liquidity

You can choose any two. If you want a high rate of return and liquidity, then you won't have principal preservation. If you want principal preservation and a high rate of return, then liquidity won't be an option. And if you want principal preservation and liquidity, then you won't have a high rate of return.

I often have clients tell me their investment accounts are diversified. But what exactly does that mean? How do they know whether they are really diversified? Some of it depends on their definition of diversified. I believe that to be truly diversified means you have to be diversified in the following four areas:

- between "principal preservation" and "growth" investment accounts across your whole investment portfolio,

- within your "growth" accounts in your portfolio,

- within your retirement **income** accounts in your portfolio, and

- between your "time horizon" and investment selections.

I'll discuss what each of these areas entails in future chapters.

Note: Some financial advisers will use the word laddering inter-changeably with diversification.

LOST IN THE FOG

It was a Saturday morning and Oliver, my 8-year-old son, and I were headed out fishing. The sky was clear and the sun was shining when we left our home, but by the time we arrived at the boat launch the fog was pretty thick.

I could see the sun trying to break through so I figured it would not be long before the fog had burned off. My plan was to get the boat in the water, stay close to shore, and just fish right near the shoreline until visibility improved.

As we started to drift into the Puget Sound, the fog started to get thicker and thicker until what had once been a very bright sun in the sky had completely disappeared. At first I thought, "Wow this sure is beautiful." It was just me and Ollie, and we couldn't see land or other boats or anything. We could hear fog horns every couple of minutes, and at one point a great big sea lion popped up about 20 feet from the boat. The water was completely calm; I was busy at work dropping our fishing gear into the water.

After I had both of our fishing poles setup, I looked up and realized I was a little disoriented. Having lost sight of the sun and land, I wasn't sure where we were. I stood up and looked at the compass. The compass said we were headed South. I have never really paid close attention to the compass before this moment, but South just didn't seem right. So I pulled up the GPS, which is several years old, and it said we were headed in the opposite direction I thought we were headed.

That didn't seem right. It was then that I started to get a little worried. At first I thought, "Well I'll just start motoring toward shore." But as we began motoring, I realized the GPS indicated we were going the wrong direction. It was so strange how I was sure we were headed one direction, but my instruments told me I was headed the wrong way. Then my imagination started to get the best of me. I started thinking, "What if my GPS goes out for some reason. Will I be able to find my way back to shore? What if this fog doesn't burn off or worse yet what if the fog keeps getting thicker." Even though I had almost a full tank of gas, I started worrying about whether the gas had been sitting too long in the tank from the last time I filled up. Was the gasoline still good? What if my motor dies out here? On and on my imagination went creating all kinds of doubt and fear. Now of course I acted as if nothing were wrong because I didn't want Oliver to be concerned, but I said to myself I need to get back to shore.

So I pulled up all our fishing gear, turned on the big motor and started following the GPS instructions to get us back to the boat launch. Really there was no reason to doubt the accuracy of my instruments, but I can tell you I was doubting them. It just didn't feel like we were headed in the right direction. Steering by GPS is a unique challenge because it takes a little time for the GPS to refresh and let me know if we were indeed going the direction we needed to.

After motoring for what seemed like eternity, but was likely only a few minutes, I saw a boat. The boat was white, and it just appeared out of nowhere. It was anchored down and not moving. Then all of a sudden I saw another boat. Again it just appeared. It is weird how the fog keeps obstacles hidden until you are right up on them. Finally we were about 15 feet from the boat launch when it came into visibility. I pulled the boat out of the water and so ended our day on the water.

As I thought back about this experience, I am reminded how fear can override our senses and make us begin to doubt all that we know is true. My instruments were accurate and following them turned out to be the best course of action, but I'm lucky I didn't let my gut instinct direct me away from following the instruments.

Having a retirement plan is a lot like having a GPS on your boat. You know which course of action you should take even when the fog rolls in and fear and uncertainty try to knock you off course.

Sometimes you just have to put faith in the fact that you made good decisions when you created the plan and know that there are going to be times when every ounce of your being believes you may be going the wrong way, but that may be when it matters the most that you stick with your plan.

Remember having a good financial plan is not for the good times. It's easy to have a great plan when everything is going great. Everyone is a genius when the stock market is rising.

Having a good financial plan is for the bad times. When disaster strikes, when your health begins to slip, when governments shutdown, when stock markets crash and when fear rules the day. These are the times when we rely heavily on the preparations made in good times so one can weather the storm and find our way when perspective or visibility is lost.

Having a good plan is like having a good GPS. The fog will roll in and create fear, doubt and uncertainty, but having the right equipment on board will guide you safely to your destination.

DEFINITIONS

Let's take a moment and define a few terms you'll see pop up throughout this book.

- **Qualified accounts** are accounts where the taxes on the invested dollars and interest earned have NOT been paid yet. The most common examples are a 401k, a 403b, an Individual Retirement Arrangement (IRA), or an employer profit sharing plan. All of these plans work in the same basic way—money earned is invested into a qualified account on a pre-tax basis. Pre-tax basis means that no taxes have been paid and the investment earns interest over time on a tax-deferred basis. It also means you'll pay taxes on these funds when you pull them out, and they will be taxed at your ordinary income tax rates and your highest tax bracket when you do.

- **Non-qualified accounts** are those where taxes are paid prior to the investment being made. This scenario means you won't have to pay taxes on the principal again when you pull it out. You will pay taxes on any capital gains, dividends and interest earned on these accounts, although this tax can be deferred until you actually pull it out of the account, depending on the financial tool you're using for investment.

- **Required Minimum Distribution (RMD)** is the minimum amount you must withdraw from tax-advantaged (qualified) retirement plans and accounts each year, beginning April 1 following the year you turn seventy-and-a-half, and by December 31 for subsequent years. These guidelines are established by the IRS and are subject to change.

- **Principal amount** is the money you originally invested before any interest or gain realized. For example, if an investor's account were valued at $10,000 USD and he or she originally had invested $6,000 USD, the principal amount would be $6,000 USD. The remaining $4,000 USD would be the gain from the investments.

- **A 1099-INT or 1099-DIV (1099)** refers to a form that reports your interest or dividend income from investments reportable to the IRS as taxable income. Investment companies are required to send these forms to investors by the end of January every year.

- **Stock market indices** are the same as a stock market index. They are indices of market prices for a particular group of stocks, such as the S&P 500 and the Nasdaq Composite Index.

- **Mutual funds** are an open-ended fund operated by an investment company that raises money from shareholders and invests in a group of assets, in accordance with a stated set of objectives. Many types of mutual funds exist, including an aggressive growth fund, asset allocation fund, balanced fund, blend fund, bond fund, capital appreciation fund, closed fund, equity fund, fund of funds, global fund, growth fund, growth and income fund, hedge fund, income fund, index fund, international fund, money market fund, municipal bond fund, prime rate fund, sector fund, specialty fund, stock fund, and tax-free bond fund.

Throughout this book, we will look at these definitions and I'll give you more explanation of many of them. If need be, you can always turn back to this section for a reminder of the definition for each term.

You'll also find a complete listing of the links and resources found in this book at **www.soundretirementplanning.com.**

Finally, before we get too far into the book, let me tell you a little about myself.

CONFESSIONS OF A FINANCIAL ADVISER

When you hear the word "confessions," automatically you think, "Oh boy, this is going to be good." Don't get too excited as my confessions are pretty GEEKY. I'm often asked, "How did you get started as a financial adviser?"

That is actually a long story, but I will point out a couple of characteristics or quirks that work as an advantage in my profession. Having a degree in business administration and having experience in banking, insurance, and the investment field for more than ten years has contributed to my success, but the roots of that success go back even further.

When I was a young boy, my dad encouraged me to start a lawn mowing business. I went around to all of my neighbors and established accounts with a few of them. I soon had more work than I could handle so I hired some of my friends in the neighborhood to help. I was eleven years old when I started and moved from that neighborhood when I was twelve. When I was eighteen and just about to start college, I reconnected with a friend and found out the lawn mowing business I had started was still going strong. That was my first business, so watching it grow and knowing that it continued to thrive after I was gone was and still is an inspiration. Thanks, dad.

I've always been a bit obsessive about my finances. When I would get my crusty dollar bills after mowing a lawn, I would take them home and wash them in the sink. I would lay them out on the counter and blow-dry them straight. I would bring them to the bank and deposit them in my savings account. At the time, that savings account was earning 10 percent. Ahh, the good old days.

I am also obsessed with numbers and counting. When I am driving down the highway, I count the number of tires on the vehicles driving in the opposite direction. Now this is pretty easy when you just have cars and trucks with four tires each, but when there are a lot of motorcycles and semi-trucks, it can really get your brain working quickly, not to mention that I am messing with the radio, wiping one of my kid's noses, handing the Chap Stick to my wife and drinking a cup of coffee…just kidding.

One last little confession, and this one works into personal finance. I love budgeting. I know this really sounds weird to many of you, but I am the dorky guy in the checkout stand at the grocery store who has to input my debits into my phone and categorize the expenses. Let me tell you, this little quirk isn't very popular in the express lane. But when tax time comes, and my CPA asks me how much I spent, I just love pulling out my computer and giving her the exact number down to the penny.

Okay, you may be thinking I'm a bit quirky, but you need to keep track of your money, monitor it, and help it grow. You also need to make your money work for you so you don't have to work for your money. Keeping track of your expenses and investments as well as planning for the future will help you focus on what you enjoy. You don't have to become a financial adviser, just someone who takes an active interest in his or her finances. You probably already have that kind of interest or you wouldn't have picked up this book, so let's get started discovering ways that you can plan for a retirement that offers you clarity, confidence and greater financial freedom.

Chapter 1

CONQUERING CHANGE

There is no shortage of knowing what to do;
there is, however, a shortage of those willing to do.
— Author Unknown

In this book, I will show you ways to create a retirement planning approach that reduces stock market volatility while providing growth, warding off inflation, and generating a lifetime cash flow.

Within the first five minutes of my educational seminars, I describe some of the common challenges or fears many people have as they transition through retirement. The biggest is the "fear of making an irreversible financial mistake."

As people age and transition through retirement, their willingness and ability to change becomes more difficult. Fear paralyzes people into inaction. They will choose to do nothing rather than confront change. In my experience, often, people don't make rational decisions about their finances or future, and that's unfortunate. Most of us tend to make emotional decisions about our money and lives. So when I present a client with a very rational reason to make a change such as diversification to reduce volatility, or using a tax-deferred or tax-free investment instead of a taxable investment, he may have a very difficult time making a decision even when the decision to change could greatly improve his situation.

One of my clients is currently eighty-nine years old. She has been widowed for years. When she was in her early eighties, her family encouraged her to move into a senior living facility. My client was opposed to this idea. She valued, as most of us do, her freedom and independence. Then a few years later, as she headed down the stairs in her home, she tripped and fell. She was in terrible pain. When I visited her in the nursing home, she told me her kids had been right and she was now going to move. Had she made the move earlier, perhaps she could have avoided this very unpleasant experience. I am happy to report that after a two-month recovery in the nursing home, she went home, packed up her life, and sold a bunch of stuff. She sold the home her husband and she had built, where they had raised their children and where she had lived for more than fifty years, and she moved into an independent senior living apartment complex. Talk about being brave.

I talk about change like it's something easy to do, but I can't imagine how hard that move must have been for her. Every time I speak with her now, she tells me how much she loves her life, and how moving out of her house was one of the best decisions she ever made. She talks about the freedom she has now to do more of what she truly enjoys, which in her case is painting and counseling. Change is the one constant in our lives, and no matter how comfortable we become, it will eventually sneak up on us and force us to grow.

The concepts I discuss in this book are going to challenge the way you have always done things. They may challenge conventional wisdom. They may challenge which financial vehicles or tools you use, and they will certainly rattle many of your most fundamental beliefs about how you have been growing and managing your money. I encourage you to temporarily suspend your pre-conceived ideas about finance and wealth management. Remember, retirement is a different animal. Even if you have accumulated great knowledge about creating wealth, a big difference exists between accumulating assets and the de-accumulation of assets. This book serves as a guide for the latter.

Education can be powerful, but only when it becomes an action. I dedicate time to writing every month, to offering free seminars, and to hosting Sound Retirement Radio to give people a greater understanding of the proper resources and tools available to them so they can make better decisions and become much more comfortable overcoming the hurdle of change.

Many of my clients are retired professionals. These sophisticated individuals have spent a lifetime developing their areas of expertise. Unfortunately and most admittedly, many of them have not had the inclination or the time to understand personal finance. Many of my clients tell me they have no desire to learn such things, so they've hired me as a professional to do it for them. Can you blame them? If I go to my doctor, I am relying on his years of expertise and training. It wouldn't make any sense for me to go back to medical school so I could spend all day diagnosing my health issues. At some point, you begin to realize that your time, not your money, is your most valuable asset, so how you spend that time becomes increasingly important as you transition through retirement.

The primary purpose of this book is to help retirees develop a plan for diversifying their assets in retirement. My goal is simple:

- Protect assets from market volatility

- Keep assets growing to outpace inflation

- Provide income for life

- Overcome the hurdle of change

Retirement is about planning for the future, for the likely, and for the unexpected. Let me give you an example. In early 2008, I foresaw the economic downturn that was approaching and tried to warn my clients about it by sending them the following email.

January 18, 2008

Dear Client:

Given the state of our economy and the turbulent market conditions, I feel this message is important. Please be sure to read it and pass it on to your friends.

When I was three years old, I remember watching a cartoon where a rabbit was being chased by a hunter. The rabbit made his great escape by dropping a banana peel, and the hunter slipped and fell, giving the rabbit plenty of time to get away. Being the curious kid that I was, I ran off to the kitchen, grabbed a banana, and ate it as fast as I could. I walked over to the basement steps, set the banana peel down, and started pushing on it with my foot. Nothing happened. Being very persistent and determined, I reached down, turned the banana peel over, pushed it with my foot as hard as I could, and sure enough, those bananas really can be slick. I fell to the basement floor and split my head open. My dad picked me up and rushed me to the hospital. Several stitches and years later, you can still see the scar in the middle of my forehead.

What's the point you ask? Well, it sure looks like our economy is standing at the top of the steps with a banana under foot. If you haven't noticed the DJIA is down over 10 percent in the last three months. Heck, it's down almost 6 percent this year alone. That is only a small part of the problem. Our national debt, sinking dollar, slowing economy, and mortgage meltdown are just a few of the other issues, and the list goes on. Frankly, this problem has more to it than I'd like to talk about in this email.

*You may want to visit **www.parker-financial.net** for more information. Feel free to call with questions.*

Hope all is well,
Jason Parker
President, Parker Financial

My job is to keep a close eye on my clients' retirement funds and investments. That's what I do, and I work hard to keep my community and clients up to speed with what's happening. "You can lead a horse to water, but you can't make it to drink." You are, ultimately, the one who has to make the hard decisions. So you have to ask yourself, "Do I really want financial help?"

I struggle with change as much as the next person. When my wife and I go out to dinner, we will go to the same restaurant because it is familiar to us. If I buy a bottle of wine, I usually go with the wine I know I like. When we go to Hawaii for vacation, we often revisit the same place. It's comfortable and safe, and we know what to expect.

Challenge yourself to embrace change. Go out to dinner tonight to a restaurant where you have never been. Start a new exercise class or join a new gym. Instead of just listening to everyone else sing at church on Sunday morning, let loose and give it your all. Do something that gets you out of your comfort zone. It will be a good exercise for you to take small steps toward change before you take the hard steps toward changing your money habits.

I recognize that changing your finances or your adviser may be a scary endeavor. And if you are happy with the results you are getting, maybe you won't need to make a change. But if you are unhappy with either the relationship you have or the results you are getting, please don't accept mediocre or poor results just because change is hard. One reason I enjoy working with retirees is because of the wisdom they bring to our relationship. I am grateful to have people in my life like the eighty-nine-year-old woman whose story I told because she is a reminder and inspiration to me about what can be accomplished. Yes, change can be scary, but even scarier is staying in a sinking ship. If the situation warrants it, be prepared to make a change.

OVERCOMING THE FEAR OF RETIREMENT

One of the top search queries bringing people to my blog is "Overcoming the Fear of Retirement." Ultimately I don't think people are really afraid of retirement, but most of us are resistant to change. A transition into the unknown can shake us out of our comfort zone and create uncertainty, which can lead to fear and stress.

I remember in late 2004, we had just found out that we were expecting our first child. My wife and I had been trying to have children for eight years. So this was amazing, wonderful, spectacular news. We were overwhelmed with joy, but, at the same time, for me there was stress associated with transitioning into the unknown. Every morning for the entire week after we found out, I'd get a bloody nose while in the shower. While we were both extremely excited and happy, I was also very nervous and fairly stressed about the responsibility of becoming a dad.

I have learned from working with many pre-retirees and retirees that the prospect of retirement can bring a similar sense of anticipation and joy. It can also cause stress and fear as people begin to prepare for the transition into the next phase of their life. Many of the people we work with have been leaders in business and in their communities. Oftentimes their identity is associated with what they do, who they've become in their career, and how much they have accomplished. Transitioning into retirement makes them realize that they are not their job. They also realize that, regardless of how much they have saved, most people are concerned it may not be enough. Now they need to redefine their identity and focus on what is truly the most important thing in their life.

There are two things I think most people could do to help themselves overcome the fear and stress of retirement: The first thing I would recommend doing is sitting down and writing out a purpose statement for this next phase of your life. I went through this process for our firm last year, and it was incredibly clarifying. The rewards of being intentional about designing your life in a way that is clear, concise, and meaningful can really provide clarity of purpose and help you decide how you will spend your most valuable asset, your time.

When I sat down to write the purpose statement for our firm I asked myself and my team three questions:

- Who are we?

- What are we going to do?

- Why are we going to do it?

You could apply these same questions to your retirement. I'll warn you that this is not an easy exercise. It took me several months to dial in our firm's purpose statement, and every word has significant meaning. Our purpose statement answers all three of these questions and is only one sentence long, so it is easy to memorize. This statement is now the foundation for every decision we make. Imagine what it would be like to wake up every morning in retirement and have that type of clarity. When you complete the process of defining your purpose statement and do the hard work of answering the three questions above, you will find that clarity.

The second thing you can do to overcome the fear of retirement is to have a written financial plan. I recommend sitting down with an adviser who specializes in working with folks transitioning into and through retirement. Finding an expert to help guide you along this path will do a couple of things: First, your adviser is not emotionally involved in the prospect of your retirement, so he or she should be able to give you objective advice. Second your adviser may know of techniques or strategies that you have not considered that have helped hundreds of others preparing for the same transition.

A good financial plan will look at your budget, cash flow, taxes, income, assets, estate planning, and insurance to help paint a picture of what your financial life will look like on a year-by-year basis as you transition into and through retirement. A good retirement plan can help answer the question, "Have we saved enough?" A plan can also help alleviate the concern of running out of money in retirement. A good retirement planner should ask you the question, "What is the purpose of this money?" You should be able to answer that question.

Hiring a qualified retirement planner can help you understand the rate of return you need to earn on your money to achieve your goals and help you craft an asset allocation, diversification, and income strategy to help you achieve that goal with as little volatility and risk as possible.

With a written financial plan for achieving your retirement lifestyle goals, you can better achieve confidence. Once you have clarity of purpose and the confidence to know the numbers are going to work, then my hope is that you will experience freedom — Freedom to do the things you want to do, to be with the people that matter the most to you, and to be free from worry, fear, and greed. Then, ultimately, may you have the freedom to make an impact in this world so that one day you might be greeted with "well done good and faithful servant."

HOPE FOR THE BEST, BUT PLAN FOR THE WORST

I remember in 2008 when I was introduced to some folks who had recently retired. They came into my office and were very concerned about their investment portfolio. They explained they had lost more than thirty percent of the value of their portfolio in less than twelve months. What was worse is they had made plans to draw income from this portfolio every year to supplement their retirement income needs.

In my industry, a prevailing bit of wisdom you may occasionally hear from financial advisers when Mr. Market is experiencing a lot of turmoil is, "Don't worry, over a long period of time the market goes up."

Or another favorite is, "Well at least you have not lost as much as ...." Either way, many people we serve are generally not comforted by this advice. Once you have retired you may not have a long period of time to recover from a significant market sell off.

I have a good friend who was heavily invested in the NASDAQ back in the year 2000. He was in his 40s at the time and had accumulated enough money to retire. But like so many people, he was earning incredible double-digit returns, so instead of taking his foot off the gas pedal of risk, he kept driving forward full speed ahead.

During what we now call the "dot-com bubble," you may have read some of the headlines where folks were quoted as saying, "I don't see any end in sight," or there is "a very powerful momentum pattern that started to form last year and is likely to remain strong." Or my favorite was business gurus calling the bubble a "True Revolution."

After the dotcom bubble burst, it wasn't until April 2015 that the NASDAQ surpassed its previous record of 5048.62. Remember the market's time horizon and your retirement time horizon may not agree. The one asset you have less of as you transition through retirement is time. The lesson learned is to always diversify your time horizon as well as your investments.

Did you know that if you lose 30 percent in one year, then you actually have to earn about 43 percent the next year just to get back to even? For example, if you have a portfolio valued at one million dollars today and you lose 30 percent ($300,000) in one year, then the next year you would start with a balance of $700,000 and would need a gain of 43 percent (approximately another $300,000) just to get back to even.

When you are drawing money out of a portfolio that is falling in value, you are making your situation much worse. For example, let's say at the beginning of the year you had an investment portfolio valued at one million dollars. The prevailing wisdom says you should be able to take a 4 percent withdrawal every year and not worry about depleting your portfolio. So at the beginning of the year you took a distribution of $40,000 from your one million dollar investment portfolio, which was the recommended 4 percent to supplement your retirement lifestyle, and then by the end of that same year you experienced a 30 percent loss.

As you began year two, your million dollars would be worth only $672,000. If, in the second year, you only take 4 percent of the now $672,000, then you would have only $26,880 of retirement income whereas the year before you had $40,000 of retirement income.

The problem is that most of the time people don't want less income every year as they transition through retirement. They generally want more income to help them keep up with rising costs. So, in this example, if the couple decides to continue to take the necessary $40,000 of income at the beginning of year two to fully fund their retirement living expenses, their $672,000 is now down to $632,000. And even though you only lost 30 percent in one year due to stock market volatility, when you also factor in the retirement income needed from the portfolio you would now require a 58 percent increase or a gain of $368,000 in your investment portfolio just to get back to the one million dollars you started with.

The problem of reverse dollar cost averaging is one of the reasons that so many retirees took longer to get back to even in their investment portfolios even though the stock market as measured by the S&P 500 has continued to post fairly strong positive returns since 2009.

When you are about to retire, be sure you make your plans based on a worst-case scenario. I've learned that it is better to plan for the worst and hope for the best than it is to plan for the best and experience the worst.

Remember that retirement is all about cash flow, not your net worth. Start your retirement journey by having a very accurate budget, calculating all of your guaranteed retirement income sources, design your retirement plan around your time horizon and not the markets, solve for your retirement income gap and create a plan that is designed to provide a high degree of certainty with the least amount of volatility. And by all means, spend your most valuable asset (your time) with the people you love, doing the things you love. If at the end of our time all we have to show is a positive balance sheet then I'm afraid we have missed our purpose.

RETIREMENT PLANNING CHECKLIST

Here is a checklist for people getting ready to retire.

- **Income:** I've learned that retirement is all about cash flow, not net worth. So one of the most important first steps is to write down all of your income sources in retirement. You will want to consider pensions from your current or past employers and Social Security benefits. Be sure to consider spousal and survivor benefits as well as explore strategies for maximizing your Social Security such as the restricted application. Examine tools such as Social Security income benefit calculators that can be found online.

- **Assets**: What assets do you have that will provide income for you? You want to consider any rental properties and provide net income. This is also where you will want to list cash, investments and retirement accounts that can be used to help you supplement your income needs.

- **Budget**: Having a good handle on your spending and knowing how much money you actually need every month to make the numbers work, will help you craft an income strategy first for your needs and second for your wants. RetirementBudgetCalculator.com is a tool we created to help you understand your spending. Use the coupon code "book" for a 50 percent discount.

- **Liabilities**: List all the people to whom you owe money. The retiree who does not owe anyone has the most flexibility and often the most comfort in retirement. A great goal before you retire is to be debt free.

- **Insurance**: Do you own Life Insurance, Long Term Care Insurance, Health Insurance, Homeowners Insurance, Car Insurance, Earthquake Insurance, an Umbrella Liability Policy, or ID Theft Protection? Which insurance do you need now that you are preparing to retire? List all of the policies you own and then talk to an independent insurance agent who can help you understand what insurance you should consider. If you are going to be turning 65 soon and planning to enroll in Medicare, be sure to check out their online tool at www.medicare.gov to help you find the best plan for your situation.

- **Estate Documents**: Are your Will, Power of Attorney, Health Care Directive, Trust and all other estate documents in good order and have they been updated recently? If not, plan to meet with an attorney to get these important documents updated.

- **Taxes**: It's not how much income you have that matters but how much of it you get to keep after Uncle Sam gets his slice. Be sure to bring your tax return to a CPA or an adviser who understands the tax code and can help you understand how much of your income is going to be taxed in retirement. It's your net after-tax income that will be the money you actually get to spend on the things that are important to you.

Chapter 2

FOCUSING ON WHAT IS MOST IMPORTANT

One of my clients once said to me, "I can spend my time losing money in the stock market, and I can spend my time making the money back in the stock market. But once I spend my time, I can never get it back."

This chapter is extremely important because it's about focusing on what is most valuable in your life, namely:

- spending your time with those you love

- learning to appreciate what you have

- being grateful

- finding peace

- being involved in your community

- taking time to pray and worship, and

- being that incredible parent, grandparent, and friend.

If you don't have your priorities straight at this stage in life, you better get going because you may not have time on your side. Many of my clients come to realize their most precious asset is their time. They could probably manage their money just as well as I can. But they don't want to do it. They want to live, and so they learn to outsource the mundane details like money management. I am not suggesting you close your eyes, hand over all your money, and forget about it. You still need to be prudent, meet regularly with your adviser, and ask a lot of questions. But chances are that if you are like most of my clients, you haven't envisioned your retirement years as sitting in front of a computer and placing stock trades all day long.

People have a lot of different reasons for hiring a money management firm or financial adviser. Sometimes it's because they don't want to become subject matter experts. Sometimes they already are experts, but they want to create the relationship to make sure that if anything happens to them, a trusted backup person is in place. Sometimes, they choose a financial adviser just to simplify their lives. When it's time to retire, some people are ready to put their feet up and relax.

You will pay fees or comissions depending on who is providing the advice, and the type of planning that is being done. Let's compare some of your options.

- **Fee for planning.** In this type of arrangement, you pay your adviser a fee annually to review your portfolio and make any suggestions and recommendations. You get a second set of eyes to look things over and make sure you aren't missing anything. Depending on the complexity of your situation, this fee will likely range anywhere from $99-$10,000.

- **Investment Management**. This style of management is appropriate for people who don't want to do all of the buying and selling required with investments. They are looking for a money manager who will watch their accounts and make adjustments as needed. Many of the people I meet with in retirement feel this assistance is prudent to have since they are no longer contributing to their retirement assets. They want an extra level of oversight to make sure their investment accounts are being managed with an eye toward optimization. You should expect to pay anywhere from 0.5 to 2 percent annually on your account value depending on the size and complexity of your accounts. Sometimes a fee-based management firm will accept commissions as a part of its compensation. This situation can be okay as long as it is disclosed up front. In my experience, mixing fees and commissions on products can be one way to reduce the overall cost to you.

- **Commission only.** In this scenario, the planner works on commission only. The more transactions the advisers complete or accounts they open, the more they get paid. These advisers are non-fiduciary in nature.

The other item to consider is whether your adviser is a fiduciary or a non-fiduciary. Federal law requires fiduciaries to act in the best interest of the client. They are required to disclose any conflicts of interest that exist. Whereas, non-fiduciaries, are only required to maintain a suitability standard. Their recommendations must only be suitable for that client's situation, needs and goals. They do not have to disclose any conflicts of interest.

One of my prospective clients delivered a book to my office a few years back. It was *The Seven Habits of Highly Effective People* by Stephen Covey. The first few pages of the second chapter of this book changed my life.

Stephen Covey introduces the principal of "begin with the end in mind" and he takes the reader through a very powerful visualization exercise. He asks you to close your eyes and imagine you just pulled up to a church. You walk inside the church and realize you are at a funeral. You walk to the front of the room look in the casket and realize it's YOU. You sit down in the front row and for the next hour you listen as family members, your spouse, children, co-workers, and community all celebrate your life. The two questions I contemplated while going through this exercise were:

- How will I be remembered?

- What have I contributed?

By figuring out what my answers currently were, and then figuring out what I wanted the answers to be, I was able to define what was most important to me, and then I started taking the steps to get me there.

Here is what I mean when I say, "Focus on what's most important." When your grandson gets up at your funeral to talk about the legacy you left, my hope is that it will be about the life lessons you taught him out on the river fishing. Nobody ever stands up and says, "My grandpa sure had a great 401k, and it was so great watching him spend all day and night reviewing his statements."

Focus on what's most important in your life and hire experts to take care of the details so you can answer the two questions above without hesitation or delay the way you want them to be answered: *"How will I be remembered?"* and *"What have I contributed?"*

CLARITY

I met with a dear client of mine today whose doctor had relayed some bad news. A couple of months ago she was diagnosed with lung cancer. This really caught her by surprise because she's been healthy her whole life, and she has never smoked. The tumor in her was growing instead of shrinking with her treatment. She will be starting a new treatment, and hopefully it works.

She had come into my office because she wanted to update the beneficiaries on her retirement accounts, based on her estate planning attorney's recommendations.

She said a couple of things that really affected me. She said the hard part about all this was the impact it is having on her adult children. I asked her if there were any big trips or anything she wanted to do with her family. She said, "No, just getting to spend as much time with them as possible. That's what it's really all about."

She said one of the great things about getting sick and knowing that you're sick is that so many people reach out to you, contact you, send you letters and come by your house to drop things by. She said, "I really feel loved." She also commented that some people aren't lucky enough to have this type of advanced warning.

It was a cold January afternoon. She looked out and said it was a beautiful day. I could just tell she really appreciated how beautiful the day was. As we were standing at her car door, the last thing she said to me was, "Jason do what you want to do. Don't wait to live."

Are you waiting to live?

LEAVING A LEGACY

I remember the time I received a call from one of my client's daughters to let me know her mom had died. My client was a very nice person with an inviting smile who was always helping her family and community. I had visited her several times in the weeks leading up to her death. The very last time I had met with her, she was no longer able to move from her chair without assistance. She said to me with her voice trembling, "I don't have much time left." She had asked me to review her estate and financial plans one last time. She wanted to know that, when she was gone, her family would be taken care of financially.

My client loved to knit, sew, and crochet. She had four children and many grandchildren. She and her husband had been very successful in business and they had raised a very close family. Whenever any of her kids or grandkids married, she would make the new couple a beautiful quilt. To accommodate all the guests, her funeral was held in a local school gymnasium. At her funeral, her friends and family draped the quilts she had made along every wall.

The thought of her legacy continues to touch me, and it reminds me of what is truly important in this life. Her faith, family, and community were her highest priorities. What may surprise you is that she also left her family a fairly large estate. But at the celebration of her life, dollar bills were not hanging from the walls—quilts were. Beautiful, handmade, exquisite quilts she had poured her heart into. That, my friends, is the type of legacy I hope all of my clients will leave.

While people make all kinds of plans and preparations to leave money or to simplify or to maximize their estates, they forget the most valuable pieces of their legacies: their personal stories of their triumphs and greatest achievements. Oftentimes, all that is left are the pictures of people's lives, the careers they had, and the dates and times they lived, but their stories are lost.

I know the Bible speaks about leaving a financial legacy, and I understand the importance, but the financial inheritance is actually the easier part. What's not so easy is taking the time to sit down and share your story. Today, the process is getting easier because of online blogs and dictation software that allow you to speak words into your computer rather than type. Let me encourage you to leave a grand legacy, one that will live forever and be more valuable to future generations than simply leaving money.

When I was twenty-one, I moved out of my dad's house. I had been dating Rebecca for more than two years. I knew she was the one for me, but she had recently moved to Alaska to finish getting her bachelor's degree. So as soon as I graduated, I decided to follow her and her family to Juneau, Alaska.

I was planning to drive from California to Seattle to put my car on the barge. I had packed all of my belongings into a large duffle sack and put a Jim Croce tape in the car for the long drive. It was really an adventure. I had said all of my goodbyes to my family and was getting into my car when my dad came outside. With tears welling up in his eyes, he gave me a big hug and said, "Good luck." Then he reached into his pocket and pulled out a silver dollar. It was dated the same year as my birth. He pressed the silver dollar into the palm of my hand and said, "Jason, since I moved out of my home, I have never had to go to my family for money. I've done it on my own, but I wanted to give you this silver dollar just in case things ever get tight."

I remember being so nervous when I was just about to get married. I felt a great sense of responsibility, and I wanted to be a good man and a good husband. A few hours before my wedding, I called my grandparents and asked them for their advice on how to have a good marriage.

My dad's mom told me, "A family that prays together stays together." My mom's parents told me, "Never go to bed mad."

My dad's mom passed away years ago. And my mom's mom passed away about two years ago. I'm grateful for their wisdom, but I wish they would have written down some of the things they had learned during their life.

Rebecca and I did get married a few years after I joined her in Alaska, and we have been together ever since. I'm so grateful that she has put up with me for all these years. We, like many people, made our mistakes with money. It's an important part of the learning process. Someone once said, "If you aren't making mistakes, you aren't living."

I am very proud of the fact that I have never had to go to my family for money. I still have the silver dollar my dad gave me years ago. There have been times when things got pretty tough for us, but that silver dollar meant so much more than just the money it was worth.

During my years of helping people plan for retirement, I have seen many families torn apart by an inheritance. I have seen brothers fall out of good favor with one another and sisters who will no longer speak to each other because of money. One of the greatest joys in my life has been learning how to become successful financially without receiving help from family or having to wonder what I will get from them.

I do not plan to leave a lot of money to my children or grandchildren because I would hate to rob them of the awesome experience of learning how to win at the game of life. And I certainly would be deeply troubled if my children fell out of favor with one another because of a large inheritance.

I suggest that you spend your money while you are alive. Create memories. Take your family on vacations and cruises. Take them out to eat. Spend the holidays with them. Create the relationships and share your wisdom. More importantly, give them the most valuable gift of all: your time.

You may plan to leave your loved ones some money, but perhaps not so much that it cripples their abilities to grow on their own. And if you want to leave something really special behind to those who will follow in your footsteps, then consider writing down a collection of your favorite quotes, a journal, blog, or even a book. It could be a wonderful gift and an amazing legacy.

MORE PERFECT MOMENTS

At a recent business luncheon we were asked to share with the group who we are, what we do, and what was our best memory from the past summer. Before you read any further, think back over last summer. What was your best memory?

One of my perfect moments from this past summer was when I was at a park with my family, and I was teaching my son how to ride his bike without training wheels. I remember the heat of the afternoon sun as I was running back in forth in the grass holding onto the back of his seat. I remember my wife and daughter sitting in the shade of a large oak tree drinking ice cold water from a translucent blue thermos. And I remember that moment when I let go of the back of my son's seat and watched as he teetered and wobbled and rode his bike for the first time with no training wheels. As I ran next to him, I looked up at my wife and with my eyes said, "Look he is doing it on his own."

As I jogged this morning, I was reflecting on the question we were asked, "What was your best memory?" and I was thinking back not just about my own best memory, but thinking about how many others in the group that afternoon answered that question. As we went around the table, almost everyone's best memory had something to do with time they spent with people they loved. Almost everyone's best memory stemmed from something they did with and for someone they cared about. It made me think that I had stumbled upon the secret formula to creating more perfect moments in my life. I was having a hard time articulating the perfect moment formula and then I picked up my Bible and read this verse: "A new command I give you: Love one another. As I have loved you, so you must love one another." John 13:34

Reading this passage made me realize the formula for more perfect moments had already been written and recorded over two thousand years ago. So while I haven't created anything new, I just wanted to share the realization I had. Perhaps one reason God wants us to love one another and serve one another is because it is in those times that we create more perfect moments.

AVOIDING FINANCIAL HARDSHIP

Two of the most challenging questions I've ever been asked were:

1. How will you be remembered?

2. What have you contributed?

After being asked those questions and contemplating the answer, I overheard someone talking about me. They said, "Jason is very driven." While I appreciated that what they said was meant as a compliment, I realized it was not what I had hoped someone might say.

A friend of mine is contemplating divorce. I am always sad and a little scared when I hear a long-time marriage is coming to an end. I'm reminded that it really takes two people to make a marriage work. I've learned that usually one person is committed to the relationship while one person wants out. As we talked, I asked him to reflect back on his past 20 years of marriage and share with me any insights on what he would have done different to try and avoid this painful place in his life. He said:

- I should have made it a priority to set aside more time to go out on dates with my wife. He said looking back he realized that she needed a little time away from the kids; time to connect with him.

- I should have created a vision for our lives with my wife and revisited that vision for our lives together on a regular basis to make sure we are on the right track and making progress toward our life goals together.

I share this with you for a couple of reasons: First, as a financial adviser, let me just say that divorce is probably the most expensive, most costly financial choice you will ever make; Second, I've read that financial strain is one of the top reasons for divorce. If you are experiencing financial hardship, then you need to be more vigilant than ever regarding your marriage. I've heard it said that often times people will leave 80 percent of something great to chase the 20 percent of something they hope they will find in someone else. Once they find the 20 percent they were looking for, they realize that the new person isn't perfect either and so they begin the search all over again. They are always searching for the missing 20 percent.

Falling in love is easy. Being in love for a lifetime is a choice and it takes work. At a summer BBQ a few years ago, I was talking with a woman whose husband had recently passed away. When it was just the two of us sitting at the table, she told me how she had a shoebox full of love letters her husband had written her over the years. Even though he was gone, she was still in love with him, and when she needed a little pick me up to be reminded of his love for her, then she would pull out one of those letters and remember.

She said to me, "Jason don't ever underestimate the importance of those little notes you write to your wife."

What I realized at that moment was that I had not written very many love letters to my wife. So after hearing her words of wisdom, I decided to take action. For one year I kept a love journal. I made it a priority to spend the first few minutes of my day to write one thing I loved about my wife. It was usually just a sentence or two about what I remembered from the day before. Over the course of the year I found something new to love about my wife every day. At the end of the year I gave the journal to my wife for our 17th wedding anniversary.

In the Bible, in Matthew, there is a verse that reads, "seek and you will find." It's amazing how we tend to find what we look for. When we focus on the good and when we choose to be grateful, it impacts our hearts in a significant and meaningful way. Learning to be content comes in part from learning to be grateful for all that we have. While keeping this journal I had thought I was writing it simply as a gift for my wife so that she would always know how important she is to me. But what I found was that in keeping this journal, I fell even more in love with her. The real gift was for me to be reminded of just how lucky I am.

If you are investing in your retirement plan, but you say you can't afford a babysitter, or a night out, or a bouquet of flowers, then I'm afraid you might end up with a lot less than you were planning for and your retirement vision could be completely lost.

If you are considering divorce, please let me encourage you to look for ways to repair your marriage. Perhaps you could begin by keeping a love journal. Love is worth it. It will be your greatest achievement, your most prized possession and your greatest legacy.

At the end of my time, if I am only remembered as a man who was driven, then I'm afraid it would not be a life very well-lived. For what is it to gain all earthly possessions, but in the pursuit of acquiring more stuff lose the relationships that matter the most? Let me encourage you to create a vision for your life. Begin with the end in mind. Invest in your relationships and plan to leave a legacy much greater than money.

FAITH, FAMILY AND FRIENDS BEFORE FINANCES

I consider myself to be relatively thrifty and for years I refused to purchase a good pair of sunglasses. I was always sitting on them, losing them, or forgetting where I left them. A few years ago my wife and I were on vacation talking, and I said, "You know I think I am finally responsible enough to own a really nice pair of sunglasses." She agreed and the rest is history.

I'm not sure if brand name sunglasses are really any better than the cheap ones, but we are proud owners of very nice sunglasses. As we prepared for a vacation to Maui over Christmas break, I mentioned to Rebecca how I was kind of surprised and proud of the fact that after several years she and I still owned the nice sunglasses we had acquired years earlier. But while on vacation during Christmas break, I was reminded that faith, family and friends come before finances and things.

One day during our vacation we were at the beach enjoying the rolling and crashing waves. Libby my 7-year-old daughter likes to play this game where I hold on to her and when a wave comes I help her jump over the wave. As we looked out with anticipation I saw the next wave rolling in and it was HUGE. I said, "Libby this one is too big. Come on we need to get out of here."

We turned and tried to start making our way back to the shore, but the current was rushing against our legs. We couldn't move fast enough. I looked back over my shoulder and realized that huge wave was just about to break right on top of us. I told her, "OK we are going to have to brace for it." I grabbed her and held on. The wave smashed us down; she went under. I was able to hold my footing at first, but then all of a sudden a second wave hit and it knocked me off my feet.

I was holding on to Libby as we both when down under the power of the waves. Heads submerged, I was struggling to hold on to my beautiful daughter as her skin was slippery from all of the suntan lotion. My expensive sunglasses were being torn from my face and in that instant I had a choice to make. Do I let go of Libby with one hand to save my sunglasses or do I hold on with both hands to pull her close. In a situation like that you don't have time to think you act on instinct.

I was holding my breath, water swirling around my head, blinded by the salt and even though she was slippery I thought there is no way I am going to let her go so I tightened my grip and pulled her close. The water finally subsided enough to let me get my footing. I pulled Libby up. I helped her to shore so she could use a towel to dry her face. We made our way up to Rebecca, my wife, who was sitting on the beach and had seen the whole thing. Rebecca was not very happy with me. Libby jokingly and sarcastically said, "Good job Dad," but shrugged it off like it was no big deal. My heart was racing, and I made my way back out into the water to look for my sunglasses.

After the adrenaline resided, and I had time to think and process this experience, I had three realizations.

First, I realized that waves are like the problems we face every day. If we turn and face them and move toward them, then we can usually get beyond the break point. Moving toward a big wave can be scary and feel unnatural, but if you can get to it and over it before it breaks on top of you, then you will be much better off. When you try to run from waves or problems, you might occasionally get away in time, but eventually you will get stuck in the perfect conditions and the problem will knock you off your feet.

Second, as I think back about this experience I asked myself how could I ever even consider my sunglasses. What is wrong with me? How could that even be a thought that would pass through my mind? But as I thought about this, I realized we all make this choice all the time. We all have to decide what is most important to us. Do we value money and stuff or relationships. I'd like to believe that given the choice all of us would choose relationships over money, but how often do we hear stories about brothers who fall out of favor with one another over an inheritance? Or marriages that end because of financial hardship?

Third, my greatest joy in life has been learning to be a dad. As a Christian becoming a dad has helped me understand what our

Heavenly Father must feel toward us. In those moments when life is crashing in on us like a rogue wave, when we make the wrong choice to try to run from a problem instead of moving toward it, when we play games and lose, when life is a struggle and challenge and we are being rolled under the force of adversity, then God in his big loving arms pulls us in close and says this is my child whom I love and I am not letting go for anything. (Hebrews 13:5 "Never will I leave you; never will I forsake you.")

I was recently asked during a radio interview what my hope for our community is as we enter the new year. My hope is that people understand their purpose. That they know what is most important to them.

Financial advisers have the responsibility of stewardship. We are tasked to oversee, protect and grow assets that reflect a lifetime of hard work and sacrifice. We also have an amazing opportunity to learn from incredible people. I've learned from the people we serve that the most important things in peoples lives aren't things. They are faith, family and friendships. My hope is that your goals for the new year reflect your priorities and that this be a year of increase for you in those areas that truly matter the most.

THE IMPORTANCE OF TITHING

I heard Dr. John Maxwell say in an interview that God created us to be a river, not a reservoir. God gives to us what He knows will flow through us.

At church on a Sunday morning, one of the pastors said that when we give, we open up space for God to come into our lives and our communities and work His miracles.

A good friend, who was known as a hard worker and earned his living in construction, had been out of work for more than two years.

What he taught me one Sunday morning changed my life.

We arrived to church a few minutes late this particular Sunday morning. The music was playing, and the congregation was standing as my wife and I walked in and found a seat. I looked over and saw my friend, let's call him Jim to protect his identity, standing with his wife. He had been on my mind a lot lately.

Being unemployed while raising his children and trying to maintain his family was taking a toll on him. He is one of the hardest working people I know. He had a great reputation for the quality of his work and his work ethic. Every once in while he would find some temporary work that would give their family a little financial boost.

This particular Sunday his wife was singing, eyes closed, hands slightly raised at her waist and tears streaming down her face. A few days earlier she had told me how she was worried about her husband. She was worried about their family and the financial strain that was taking an emotional toll.

When the music stopped, the pastor gave a quick introduction and the elders of the church began passing around the offering plate. As the offering plate came to Jim and his wife, I saw her write a check and place it in the offering plate.

My heart sank.

My good friend who had been unemployed, struggling to find work, under a strain because of the financial burden was placing money in the offering plate.

Up until this point my wife and I had never been very good tithers. We would give small amounts of money here and there but never regularly and never very much.

I was humbled by our friend's obedience in tithing at time when he did not have a lot to give. My heart was touched that Sunday and on the drive home from church my wife and I talked, and we came up with a dollar amount that we decided to start tithing on a regular basis.

What makes this so hard and embarrassing is that we had been very blessed in our finances. Our company was experiencing incredible growth. We were saving a lot, and we were taking amazing family vacations. Tithing was not a concept I understood; any little bit I gave was very hard for me. No matter how much money we made, no matter how much we saved, I never felt like we had enough to be able to tithe.

After a few months of tithing at the level we had originally agreed to, I realized that we were short-changing God by 50 percent. I knew that the Bible instructed us to tithe 10 percent of our income. I realized that we were only tithing 5percent.

For a family who had not tithed on a regular basis up to this point, the 5percent tithe was uncomfortable for me. But I remember thinking if I am ever audited by God, then I don't want to explain why I decided to only give half of what he asked of us. So after a few months we increased our tithe to 10 percent.

My hand would shake and I would let out a sigh every month I would write that tithe check. I'd pray, "Dear Lord help me depend on you." But after I would write the check, I remember feeling a sense of calm; a sense of peace. I was beginning to let go of the idol I had made money into.

Time passed and I was sitting with my CPA in December looking at our personal and business finances for the year. My tithe had been constant every month at 10 percent of the amount of salary I paid our family. We had a good year in business and there were a few opportunities for us to give an offering above our tithe. This was the most our family had ever given in tithes and offerings in one year. I began to feel my hands opening and releasing control. I was shifting from grasping and holding on so tight to every dollar to realizing God was in control, and I was learning to depend on Him.

As I was working with our CPA, she tallied up our tithes and offerings for the year. She then calculated our net profit for our company. When she told me what our net profit was, I realized that our tithe and offerings that year matched almost exactly to the penny 10 percent of my company's net profit.

Because I was tithing 10 percent of my salary and not based on what the profit of the company was, I was surprised to see that the correlation between my tithe and our companies profit was so close.

Another year went by. We continued to tithe our 10 percent but the offerings we made the second year were a little bit less. Once again December arrived, and I was sitting with our CPA. Once again she tallied our tithes and offerings and then our net profit from our company. Our tithes and offerings had decreased that year and so had our net profit. Once again the amount we gave worked out to be almost exactly to the penny 10 percent of what my company's net profit was for the year.

The first year this happened, I thought it was a fun coincidence. But the second year this happened, I almost fell out of my chair. Having this happen a second year really captured my thoughts and around this time I read the verse Malachi 3:10:

> "Bring the whole tithe into the storehouse, that there may be food in my house. Test me in this," says the LORD Almighty, "and see if I will not throw open the floodgates of heaven and pour out so much blessing that there will not be room enough to store it."

I know this sounds crazy but I felt like God was saying Jason, "You can trust me. I will keep my end of the bargain if you will trust me."

This verse in Malachi says to test me in this. Well I asked my pastor friend about that because there is another verse that says to never test God. He explained this to me so simply. He said, "Jason don't test God, except in this one area."

In our third year of tithing I decided to test God. I began tithing 20 percent of my salary. The past two years God had been faithful. I was wondering if our tithe and our companies profit were somehow linked. I was wondering if this had all just been a happy coincidence or if there was something more to this.

In December of that third year, when I was sitting with my CPA, I knew my business had the best year we ever had. We tallied our tithes and offerings, and then she tallied our net profit.

Within a few pennies our tithe was 10 percent of our net profit.

I remember getting goosebumps. I was almost in tears as I exclaimed, "WOW." I shared with my wife what had happened.

What made this even more remarkable was we had decreased our number one marketing strategy budget by half at the same time, and our profit still increased. That doesn't make financial sense, but God's ways are not our ways. His ways are higher than our ways.

Tithing has been one of the hardest things I have ever learned. It has helped me to believe that I can trust God. That He is good for his promises.

I've learned that tithing is not about money, but it is about where you place your trust.

I've learned that when you are uncomfortable in your faith, then your eyes are opened and you can see things you may not have otherwise seen.

I have learned that my treasure is not in my bank account. My treasure is in Heaven and that is where I want my heart to be.

My friend taught me that it is not our money that we should trust in. When you trust God by tithing what you are saying is that you have more confidence in what God will do in your life then what money will do.

I'm also reminded that people are always watching us.

People watch how we live our lives and that it is not about what we say, but what we do that matters.

Watching my friend tithe that Sunday morning changed my life. He has never said a word to me about being faithful or tithing. We have never talked about this story. Through his actions, his trust, and his example, I'm beginning to learn what stewardship means and what it means to trust in God.

My family gave at a time that we had an abundance.

But he gave when he did not have the extra to give.

I was reluctant to share this story because I don't want to bring attention to our family's tithing. At the same time I want to share God's goodness, God's faithfulness and encourage others to depend more on Him. I also believe that sharing our faith journey is a family legacy. I think future generations of my family should know about the foundation that we build our lives upon.

My friend Frank Reed has helped teach me about tithing. He wrote a book called, *In God We Trust, Dollars and Sense.* This is a good book if you would like to learn more about the importance of tithing.

As always, the best resource is the Bible. To quote the book of Luke 12:34, "Wherever your treasure is, there the desires of your heart will also be."

I've been collecting scripture that relates to stewardship and tithing. Visit **www.soundretirementplanning.com** and search for "Tithe" to read some of the verses around this topic.

Chapter 3

CAN I AFFORD TO RETIRE?

Our prospective clients often ask, "Can I afford to retire?" My team has found that retirement is all about cash flow, not net worth. Especially after the real estate crash, we have met people who may have a net worth of $2 million, which looks great on paper, but when it comes to retirement income, they are just barely squeaking by on their Social Security and a small pension. It's great that you are worth $2 million, but ultimately, it's your cash flow that will determine your quality of life in retirement, not your net worth.

The most successful retirees we know have learned to live within their means. It's critical that you establish your budget so you can accurately determine how much retirement income you are going to need. The first goal of a good retirement income plan will be to guarantee anywhere from 70 to 100 percent of the income needed to maintain your basic living needs on an inflation adjusted basis.

MEASURE TWICE CUT ONCE RETIREMENT PLAN

In the world of retirement planning you would be amazed how many people make a cut before measuring. When preparing for retirement the very first step should be to create a retirement plan not an investment strategy.

We are in the process of remodeling our kitchen. My wife has been working hard, and she is doing an amazing job lining up the right contractors, getting multiple bids, picking out all of the colors and designing an amazing space.

One of her best decisions so far was to hire Kristy Ludwig (Kristy Ludwig Kitchen and Bath Co.) to help with kitchen & cabinet design. Kristy has years of experience and her family owns a cabinet making company (Markay Cabinets, Inc.) so she is very knowledgeable in both materials, design and function. Before the cabinets were constructed, Kristi met with my wife several times to go over specifics and details. They spent several hours together designing a beautiful kitchen that would utilize and maximize our space.

When I was a boy working on a home project with my Dad, he once told me to "measure twice and cut once." I agree with him that it is better to take your time upfront and do the job right the first time around than to hurry and possibly make mistakes wasting materials. He said, "Jason once you make the cut you can't take it back." One of the things I noticed about working with Mrs. Ludwig is that she measured multiple times before sending the final plans to the cabinet makers for production. Her diligence gave us a tremendous amount of confidence in her work.

Can you imagine if our kitchen/cabinet designer did not take the time to make proper plans? What would have happened if we walked into her office and she designed our new kitchen without ever measuring our home or asking us what we wanted? Wouldn't that seem crazy? How much confidence would we have in the final outcome?

We've learned from working with hundreds of retirees that retirement is all about cash flow. You need to begin your retirement journey by understanding how much money you spend every month and then looking at how much income you have coming from guaranteed sources such as social security and pensions. You'll also need to consider the impact inflation will have on your plan over time. In addition, married couples need to consider what cash flow will look like if one person dies and how a significant health care event might impact their financial well being.

If you are like most people we meet with, then chances are pretty good the reason you have saved money over the years is to help supplement your income needs in retirement. You likely want to travel, spend time with those you love, doing what you love, and you want to avoid ever becoming a burden to your family either physically or financially.

Too many people today are creating an investment strategy and diversification strategy before they create a retirement plan. How could you create a plan for investing your life savings without understanding the impact of the overall plan?

A good retirement plan should be your foundation for making financial decisions. A comprehensive plan will provide you with strategies for maximizing your social security income. It should compare your guaranteed cash flow versus your budget and identify any income gaps. A well-developed retirement plan can help you understand the minimum rate of return you need to earn to make the numbers work and help you craft a strategy for dealing with the health care risks you might experience. Finally, it should take into consideration the volatility of the stock market. Once all of those fundamental components have been explored, then you have the data you need to create a retirement income plan, diversification strategy and investment strategy.

In a recent interview on CNBC, Robert Schiller, who won the Nobel Prize in economics in 2013 and is considered one of the 100 most influential economists in the world, said that in some markets housing, stocks and bonds all seem expensive. He said, "The whole thing might correct down both bonds and stocks." In a recent interview in This Is Money, Mr. Schiller said the current CAPE is 26.3 (compared to the average of 15.21 for the 20th century according to Wikepedia). He went on to say there have only been three major occasions since 1881 where the CAPE was higher. The years were 1929, which was followed by the great depression; 2000, which we now call the tech bubble; and 2007 commonly called the financial crisis or great recession. Mr. Schiller is well known for the CAPE ratio (Cyclically Adjusted Price to Earnings), which helps investors understand if equity markets (S&P 500) are a bargain or expensive by dividing price by the average 10 years of earnings adjusted for inflation. A high

CAPE value would indicate stocks are expensive and a low number indicates stocks are a bargain.

This information is not to scare you. Instead I hope to empower and encourage you to stress test your portfolio. If we were to experience a market crash how would that impact your retirement plan? Do you have a retirement plan? This is especially important if you or someone you know is getting ready to retire. Please join with us and share this information with the people you care about. Ten thousand people a day are retiring in our country and from my experience most people have an investment strategy but few have a retirement plan. Hoping for the best is not a plan. This may seem like common sense advice, but from what we've experienced this is not common practice. It does not need to be complicated. Just remember "Measure twice, cut once."

STRESS TEST YOUR RETIREMENT PLAN

On October 23, 2014 the Federal Reserve issued the supervisory scenarios that will be used to stress test banks. Their press release stated, "The aim of the annual reviews is to ensure that large financial institutions have robust, forward-looking capital planning processes that account for their unique risks, and to help ensure that they have sufficient capital to continue operations throughout times of economic and financial stress ..."

Under the most severely adverse scenarios, the federal reserve will test banks to see how they might hold up under hypothetical conditions. These are not forecasts. Some of the hypothetical conditions are:

- Unemployment rising to 10 percent

- Equity prices drop by 60 percent

- House prices drop by 25 percent

- A rise in oil prices to $110 dollars a barrel.

The aim of a good retirement plan is to help you have a forward-looking, capital-planning process that accounts for your unique risks to help ensure that you will have sufficient capital so that you won't run out of money in retirement, never become a burden physically or financially to your family and that your financial strategy will continue through times of economic and financial stress. Have you ever considered stress testing your own investment portfolio and retirement plan?

In 2008, we met a couple who shared with us that they had experienced a 49 percent drop in their investment portfolio during the financial crisis. Before the financial meltdown, they had an investment portfolio valued at 1 million dollars. They were in their mid 60s at the time, and their financial adviser had told them they could draw out 4 percent per year without having to worry about running out of money. Four percent of 1 million dollars is $40,000. They had built their lifestyle expectations around that income. By the time they came into my office for a second opinion, their 1 million dollars had eroded to about $500,000. This couple hand a very difficult decision to make. Should they reduce their income to reflect the current value of their portfolio? Or should they continue to take the income they needed and significantly increase the probability of running out of money?

The prudent person will want to stress test their retirement plan. While the methodology may vary, the principles are similar and should include:

- How would a significant health care event that required a prolonged level of care impact your financial well being?

- What if your spouse dies, and then you experience a decrease in pension and social security income?

- How might your investment portfolio perform under different macro economic scenarios?

- Are you being too conservative with your mix of investments? Or are you being too aggressive?

- How might a low rate of return or severe market correction impact your financial well being?

- If you own bonds or bond mutual funds, then how will increasing interest rates impact your portfolio?

- How will inflation impact your purchasing power over time?

Many investment advisers have the ability to run forward-looking stress tests of both an individuals retirement plan and their investment strategy to uncover individuals risks. Every investment portfolio contains risks and by using forward-looking macro economic stress testing models you can begin to formulate what if scenarios and explore proactive solutions.

A comprehensive retirement plan considers risks to mitigate, opportunities to capture and is more than a risk tolerance questionnaire and an investment diversification strategy.

Consider this quote from one of the recent guests I interviewed on my weekly radio show, "Without income there is no retirement."

If you are thinking of retirement, then be sure to start the journey by creating a great retirement income plan. Married couples should know the strategies to maximize their social security benefits and have a good handle on how much they spend every month on basic living expenses.

In years past the general wisdom was to allocate more money to bonds and less to stocks as you grow older. The idea was that bonds were safer than stocks. Much of this advice is based upon past performance of how bonds and bond mutual funds have historically performed. The problem we have today is that the economic landscape looks much different going forward that it did in the past. We have been in a falling interest rate environment for 30 years, which helped make bonds an attractive investment from a historical standpoint because they produced income and capital appreciation as interest rates fell. With the fed funds rate sitting at zero and ten year treasury notes currently paying less than three percent, the prudent investor should be asking if bonds will provide the downside protection in their portfolios going forward that they have in the past.

Designing your retirement plan based on what has happened in the past would be like driving your car while only looking in your rearview mirror. A good retirement plan should consider what has happened in the past, but also have a forward-looking approach. The prudent retiree should conduct a comprehensive "Stress Test" on their retirement plan.

BEFORE YOU RETIRE: 3 IMPORTANT CONSIDERATIONS

One of the advantages of being a financial adviser who specializes in working with pre-retirees and retirees is I get unique insights into both the benefits and regrets of retirement planning. Based on those insights please consider the following before you retire.

1) Purchasing or refinancing a home

Remember banks lend money based on your income, not your assets. We recently met with some folks who retired in their mid 50s. They will be living primarily off their savings until their pensions and social security income starts in their 60s. Unfortunately, they did not refinance their home while they were working and had good income. Even though interest rates have dropped, they are not in a position to refinance their mortgage because banks want to see a history of income before making a loan. Drawing interest and dividends from an investment portfolio is not looked upon favorably by lenders unless you have at least two years of income history from that source. So be sure to refinance or purchase your retirement home while you still have good income. If you have already retired, then you might consider using a single premium immediate annuity (SPIA) to generate income over a five-year period of time. The banks will look more favorably at income from a guaranteed SPIA contract than they would monthly draws from a money market account.

2) Budgeting for individual health insurance

One of the biggest expenses facing people who retire early is the monthly expense for health insurance. Not too long ago, we met with a couple who retired in their late 50s; who did not research and understand the full cost of health insurance before they retired. Many people's employers provide their health insurance so they are not aware of the cost for individual health insurance plans.

Currently, a married couple in their late 50s, in Kitsap County, could be looking at monthly premiums for a high deductible HSA-qualified health plan that would start at $920 per month based on an $8,000 family deductible per year for the couple. The premiums would increase as deductibles decrease.

Federal health insurance premium tax credits do exist that may help reduce your out-of-pocket insurance premiums when you purchase the insurance through the government healthcare exchange. For example, if we use the same information for the couple above, then they would be eligible for a health insurance premium tax credit based on their modified adjusted gross income (MAGI). If their MAGI for the year was $55,000, then they would receive a $704 per month tax credit toward their premiums, and their out-of-pocket insurance premium would be reduced to $219 per month. If their MAGI was $63,000, then they would have to shoulder the entire $920 per month since they would not eligible for any of those tax credits. Please keep in mind, these amounts will change over time and premiums are based on where you live.

Remember that income from a Roth IRA is tax free and is not counted toward your MAGI. If you are over age 59.5, have met the 5 year holding requirement and the distribution counts as qualified (non-taxable), then you may want to consider taking some of your retirement income from your Roth IRA instead to ensure your MAGI remains below the threshold to qualify for the premium tax credit. Also if you have health insurance through an employer plan (or former employer) or buy it privately then there is no credit to be had. All of this is subject to change based on the political agenda of those leading our country.

3) Creating a cash flow plan

Retirement is all about cash flow not your net worth. Without income you do not have retirement. Your income will determine your lifestyle in retirement so you need to understand exactly how you will meet your income needs. A good retirement cash flow plan should start with a good budget to fully understand how much money you spend every month/year. You should make conservative assumptions about future inflation and the rate of return at which your money will grow. Remember the sequence of returns within your portfolio can make or break your plan.

If you experience a significant loss in the year you retire, then it may be devastating to your overall future cashflow. You should also take into consideration your health and your family's history of longevity to make informed decisions about when and how to start social security and pension income.

If you are married, then you should also consider the impact on your cash flow if one spouse were to pass away or have an extended medical issue that required ongoing treatments or care not covered by traditional health insurance or medicare. We've learned the more conservative an income plan that covers that gap between your guaranteed income and your budget, the more confidence people tend to have as they transition through retirement.

We can all learn from one another. There is a collective intelligence in specialization. You do not have to plan for retirement alone. Find someone who you can trust who specializes in retirement planning, and get a second opinion. "An ounce of prevention is worth a pound of cure." Sometimes an outside perspective can help you see things that you may not be trained to see.

8 CRITICAL RETIREMENT PLANNING MISTAKES TO AVOID[1]

Planning for retirement is important, and below are 8 critical retirement planning mistakes that we believe you should avoid.

1. **Not having a cash flow plan:** Retirement is all about cash flow not your net worth. Without cash flow you do not have a retirement. Your income will determine your lifestyle in retirement. Now that you are retiring, what you have accumulated needs to provide for your income needs for the remainder of your life. Spending too much in the early years or experiencing significant losses in the early years could result in you running out of money before you run out of time.

---

1   **Links used when researching this chapter.**
- http://www.multpl.com/shiller-pe/
- http://www.rwjf.org/content/dam/farm/reports/issue_briefs/2014/rwjf410654
- https://www.genworth.com/corporate/about-genworth/industry-expertise/cost-of-care.html
- http://financeandinvestments.blogspot.com/2015/01/historical-annual-returns-for-s-500.html
- http://data.bls.gov/pdq/SurveyOutputServlet
- http://www.federalreserve.gov/faqs/economy_14400.htm

2. **Not having a budget.** Many high net worth/high income earners have never lived on a budget. Because their wages are high, they have just lived comfortably and been able to save along the way. When you retire you no longer have earned income. Now what you have saved needs to provide for you. To create a good cash flow plan in retirement you need to have a good handle on how much money you spend every month and year. Underestimating your budget could throw off all of the calculations you make when creating a retirement plan. The more accurate your budget, then the better your cash flow plan. We developed *Retirement Budget Calculator* as a tool to help you know where your money is going. When it comes to living on your budget, I prefer the old fashioned envelope system. Benjamin Franklin once wrote, "A small leak will sink a great ship." Create a budget before your retire and practice sticking to it.

3. **Not maximizing Social Security.** For many people Social Security retirement income will represent 40 percent or more of their guaranteed retirement income. Social Security is tax-advantaged income, inflation adjusted and has spousal and survivor benefits that need to be considered. A poor choice when starting social security could result in $50,000 or more of lost benefits and could be the difference between having enough money to last the rest of your life or running out of money too soon.

4. **Having debt:** To quote the Bible, "The borrower is slave to the lender." If you envision retirement as a time of freedom, travel, spending time with loved ones and service to others,

then having debt may hinder your dreams and your sense of confidence. We've found that some of the most successful retirees pay cash when buying used cars; pay off credit cards every month and only justify using them at all as a means of accumulating travel rewards; and, in the best case situations, have paid off their mortgage.

5. **Assuming unrealistic stock market rates of return:** Since 1926 the stock market, as measured by the S&P 500, has averaged annualized returns a little more than 10 percent. (This represents historical performance only, and is not a predictor of how the market will perform in the future.) The key to these returns is time. Over shorter periods of time, the stock market can trade sideways or negative. Assuming constant rates of returns of 7-10 percent may make your retirement numbers look good, but may not be realistic given your retirement time horizon. If you are thinking of buying stocks today, then you should take to into consideration that the S&P 500 looks expensive relative to history when using price-to-earnings on a cyclically adjusted basis. With yields on 10 year treasuries yielding less than three percent, I'd say bonds are also looking expensive on a historical basis. When making assumptions about future rates of return, I like to say, "Let's hope for the best, but plan for the worst."

6. **Not planning for long-term health care costs:** Most people will be eligible for Medicare when they turn 65 and many will choose to purchase a supplemental policy to cover the 20 percent of health care costs that Medicare does not cover. However, this still results in potential gaps in coverage

especially for health care needed for an extended period of time. These are the types of health care events that don't kill you, but require you to need some assistance for an extended period of time. They can be brought on by stroke, heart attack, cancer, dementia, Alzheimer's, Parkinson's, MS and the list goes on. That is where long term care insurance comes in. According to Genworth's website, a recent study shows that 70 percent of people over 65 will need some type of support over their lifetime. In the United States, the average monthly cost for a private nursing home room was $8,121per month in 2017. Many people I've met with don't want to believe that any of these things could ever happen to them. They point to their good eating habits, healthy lifestyle choices, family history and argue that they will never end up needing assistance. While no one wants to think about how our health could change or about possibly losing our independence, not planning for this type of health care expense could significantly strain, if not completely wipe out, a retirement plan. Worse it may lead to adult children having to consider becoming caregivers. There is an old saying that says, "One momma can take care of eight babies, but eight babies can't take care of one momma."

7. **Not planning for inflation:** Ask anyone who retired with a fixed pension 20 years ago about inflation, and you will get an earful. During the last 100 years, inflation has averaged 3.15 percent as measured by CPI and during the past 10 years has averaged 1.75 percent. The Federal Reserve has an inflation target of 2 percent over the medium term. When planning

for your future income needs, be sure you are taking into consideration the fact that your dollars will purchase less in the future than they do today. Create a plan that assumes you will need more dollars to maintain your lifestyle needs in future years.

8. **Not having a plan for when one spouse dies:** Oftentimes with married couples one person manages the household and one person manages the finances. Unfortunately when the one spouse who manages the finances passes away or experiences a significant health event, the well spouse can be left in a fog of uncertainty about what they should do, where things are and what should happen next. Not only do you need to make sure the surviving spouse will have enough income to maintain their lifestyle, but also the surviving spouse needs to be able to have the confidence to be able to continue to carry on the plan that was originally created.

INFLATION & YOUR RETIREMENT

One of our clients brought by a ledger his mother kept from January through February 1956. His mom was trying to track where all their money was going because they had no idea why they didn't have enough left at the end of every month. What's fascinating to me about this ledger is the impact inflation has had over the last 57 years. Here are a few items from this 1956 ledger that caught my attention: rent $40 per month; car payment $44 per month; gas & electric $11 per month; groceries about $80 per month; black and white TV payment $13 per month and a swamp cooler payment of $6 per month. Their income was $77 per week; $309 per month; $3,706 per year. When I plug some of these numbers into the Bureau of Labor statistics inflation calculator, I found that $40 for rent in 1956 would be $342 today.[2]

I can't imagine a family could find a home to purchase or rent at $342 per month today. An annual income in 1956 of $3,706 is the equivalent income in 2013 of $31,712. Here are the other expenses in today's dollars: car payment $376, gas & electric $90, groceries $685, black & white TV $111, swamp cooler $51.

Historically inflation has been directly related to the increase in the quantity of money. When the Federal Reserve Bank slashes the federal funds rate and uses tools such as quantitative easing, the federal reserve is increasing the quantity of money to produce inflation. Milton Friedman, who won the Nobel prize in economics, once said, "There has never in history been an extremely rapid increase in the quantity of money without an inflation."[3]

With the Federal Reserve slashing rates and buying assets, they have injected trillions into the system. In the USA where we are running a budget deficit[4] with debt that is growing exponentially, most people would argue that the $2.5 trillion dollars the fed has injected into the system would meet the definition of a rapid increase in the quantity of money.[5] However, when I spoke with Steve Cunningham who is the director of

2 http://www.bls.gov/data/inflation_calculator.htm. Accessed February 6, 2014.

3 http://www.usdebtclock.org/. Accessed February 6, 2014.

4 http://youtu.be/NgSqZKx0mNI. Accessed February 6, 2014.

5 http://money.cnn.com/2013/05/01/news/economy/federal-reserve-stimulus/index.html. Accessed February 6, 2014.

research for the American Institute for Economic Research[6] he said, "Even though the federal reserve has been increasing the money supply, much of that money supply is sitting in banks reserves. And banks, at the time we're writing this, are holding fifteen times excess reserves. It is when banks begin to release the money back into the system that the money supply increases and the effects of inflation may begin to take hold."

Milton Friedman[7] taught that historically a lag existed between the time the money supply increased and inflation took hold.[8] With banks holding 15 times excess reserves, you have to wonder what impact it will have on prices if all of that money begins to flow into the economy. The fact that we have not yet experienced inflation due to the federal reserves quantitative easing may just be the lag Milton Friedman lectured on.[9]

One of the challenges we have when working with trillions of dollars is that it's hard for most of us to wrap our minds around just how much money that is. To give you some perspective, if you gave away one million dollars per day it would take you 2,738 years to give away one trillion dollars. Jesus walked the earth about 2,000 years ago. So you would have had to start giving away one million dollars per day 738 years before Jesus was born just to get to one trillion dollars.

6 https://www.aier.org/. Accessed February 6, 2014.

7 http://youtu.be/u6GWm0GW7gk. Accessed February 6, 2014.

8 http://youtu.be/6W_9I0nk8uI. Accessed February 6, 2014.

9 http://youtu.be/NgSqZKx0mNI. Accessed February 6, 2014.

A dollar in hand today will purchase more than a dollar will purchase in the future, and this is not by accident but by design. As you transition into retirement you need to realize having too much money safe secure and guaranteed may make you feel good in the short term, but sitting in a large cash position is likely a recipe for losing purchasing power over time. According to **www.bankrate.com**, a five year CD (Certificate of Deposit) is currently paying 1.98 percent. So if inflation is currently running at 1.5 percent, and you have to pay ordinary income tax of 15 percent on the interest you earn in your CD at the end of every year, then you can see the 1 percent you earn in your CD is slowly losing purchasing power. One of our clients recently quipped that CD stands for certificate of disappointment because of the dismal rates. Most of the people we meet don't like the idea of having to cut back on their lifestyle every year as they transition through retirement. This is why you need to keep your money working hard for you.

What steps should you take right now to position your money and protect your purchasing power if inflation is getting ready to hit? In a summary of a working paper by the Yale International Center for Finance titled, Facts and Fantasies About Commodity Futures, dated February 2005 and then updated May 2015[10], the researchers point to commodities as one possible way to diversify your portfolios against inflation. The researchers wrote:

"Commodity futures returns have been especially effective in providing diversification of both stock and bond portfolios. The correlation with stocks and bonds is negative over most horizons,

10 https://papers.ssrn.com/sol3/papers.cfm?abstract_id=2610772. Accessed July 2018.

and the negative correlation is stronger over longer holding periods. We provide two explanations for the negative correlation of commodity futures with traditional asset classes. First, commodity futures perform better in periods of unexpected inflation, when stock and bond returns generally disappoint. Second, commodity futures diversify the cyclical variation in stock and bond returns."

If you're not familiar with the term commodities think of items such as energy (oil & gas), grains (corn & wheat), precious metals (gold & silver), industrial metals (high grade copper), livestock (hogs & cattle), as well as "soft goods" such as cocoa, coffee, cotton and sugar. Commodity futures have a reputation for being risky, and you shouldn't invest in anything unless you understand all of the risks. Today investors are looking to tools such as mutual funds, ETFs and annuities that invest in or are linked to commodities to give them some exposure to this riskier asset but further diversifying their portfolios. Ultimately if you are concerned about protecting your purchasing power, then you may want to consider diversifying your portfolio by owning real assets which have historically done well during inflationary times.

We are in a unique economic environment and past performance is no guarantee of future results. Commodities are just one way investors are looking to diversify their portfolio. Many are also considering tools such as TIPS (Treasury Inflation Protected Securities), dividend paying stocks and inflation protected annuities.

Retirement is all about cash flow not your net worth. Your income and purchasing power is what will allow you have the lifestyle you have worked hard for. Your retirement plan should include strategies for trying to reduce the risk of stock market volatility, protect your purchasing power from the effects of inflation and generate a lifetime of inflation adjusted income as securely as possible.

BUDGETING IN RETIREMENT

We recently met with some affluent and successful retirees who came to see us with some questions on cash flow. They had incomes of more than $100,000 per year, yet they felt like they didn't have enough income to enjoy the lifestyle they had grown accustomed to. We asked them to tell us the very first thing that comes to mind when they hear the word "budget." One said it had a negative connotation and meant having to cut back. The other one said budgeting was financial discipline and being prudent. Most of us would probably agree with one of these two statements.

With all the nonstop chatter in Washington, D.C. these days about sequestration and budgeting, the last thing you probably want to read is an article about budgeting. This topic tends to make most people cringe. One of the things we've learned by working with very successful and very wealthy people is that it doesn't matter how much money you make or how much income you have because many people tend to increase their lifestyle expectations as quickly as their income increases. A good friend of mine is fond of saying that the luxuries of the past become the necessities of today, and sometimes the most difficult part of budgeting for a married couple is getting both people to agree upon a budget.

Budgeting is simply taking the time to make a conscious, disciplined decision about how you will spend your money. The alternative is to spend your time wondering where your money went. During our years of accumulating wealth many of us budget so we can save more. But once you have retired, the emphasis isn't so much on trying to save as much as possible as it is trying to figure out how much you can spend without having to worry about running out of money. Budgeting in its most basic sense is simply an exercise of comparing your income vs. expenses.

The easy part of a budget is understanding how much income you will have. But as you prepare to transition into retirement, you will need to have a solid handle on how much money you spend every month. Doing so will help you determine if you have saved enough to support your retirement lifestyle goals and give you a foundation for structuring an income plan. It will also provide you with the confidence that you will not run out of money in retirement.

Most people have a hard time carrying around a notebook and recording every penny they spend. So if you are comfortable using technology, then you may want to consider a program like **www.RetirementBudgetCalculator.com**. One of the advantages of tracking your spending, using a tool like *Retirement Budget Calculator*, is that it makes it easy to discover where every penny is being spent. When you mix cash into the equation, then creating an honest assessment of just how much you are spending on the little things becomes difficult, and sometimes the little things are what can create big problems. Benjamin Franklin said it best, "Beware of the little expenses; a small leak will sink a great ship."

Now I know some of you are thinking "This is just a little too Big Brotherish for me." The nice thing about *Retirement Budget Calculator* is it does not require any account numbers. I have been very pleased with how this budgeting tool works. It's always a shocker to see just how much of my money my local grocery store, Central Market in Poulsbo, is getting. If this method seems a little too high tech for some of you, and you'd prefer using a good old-fashioned paper budget data-gathering form, then I have included one on our website at **www.soundretirementplanning.com** on the resources page.

Your goal when developing your personal monthly budget is to get a solid grasp of how much money you need every month to pay for basic living expenses. Take into consideration any bills you pay quarterly, semi-annually, or annually such as property taxes and insurance. Once you have a clear picture of just how much you need every month, then you can start to have some fun and find out how much more you want for things like travel, play, and spoiling your grandkids.

Our government has a good track record of making sure our dollars have less purchasing power every year. If you visit the Bureau of Labor and Statistics inflation calculator, then you will find that $10,000 dollars in 1970 has the same purchasing power as $65,870 in 2018. So while you may need $6,000 per month in 2018 to have the desired lifestyle, you need to make sure your income plan is flexible enough to be able to adjust to rising costs in future years.

While most people focus on maximizing their income, we've also had the good fortune of working with some folks who choose to take a hard look at reducing expenses. One couple in particular comes to mind. They wanted to reduce their expenses, but didn't want to reduce their standard of living. After two years of research and travel, they decided that their dollars would stretch much further by living abroad than they would by living in Kitsap County. Today they enjoy a moderate climate in what's known as an expatriot community where people from all over the world retire. They say the culture is great, and the weather is incredible. Everyone who lives in their community is a transplant from around the globe, and they are looking to make new friends so they have a vibrant social life. They have a better lifestyle at a fraction of the cost. Email us at **info@soundretirementplanning.com** with the subject "Living Abroad" to listen to an interview regarding this topic.

Ultimately, a budget allows you to understand your basic expenses so that you can construct an income plan to help you get every ounce of life out of the dollars you have accumulated. Retiring without a budget is like taking a road trip without a map. You may reach your destination, but the trip will likely be expensive, wasteful, and create a lot of unnecessary worry.

VOLATILITY AND YOUR TIME HORIZON

You have probably heard the saying, "Don't worry; the market goes up and down, but over a long period of time it goes up." However, it's important to understand your time horizon versus the market's time horizon.

Retirees start to question this age-old wisdom when the market takes a turn for the worse like it did in 2008 because they realize they may not have fifteen, twenty, or even thirty years for the market to hopefully recoup. If you are relying on your investment portfolio to generate an income stream to supplement your other retirement income, it becomes increasingly important to be protected against such volatility.

I recently ran an online calculator for a male, age seventy, to determine life expectancy. His life expectancy was eighty-three, which establishes a basic time horizon to work with. Now we can start building a retirement strategy around some reasonable assumptions. If these numbers are correct, should he have 100 percent of his assets in growth stocks if the purpose of the money is to generate consistent and reliable income? No.

Below is a chart of the Dow Jones Industrial Average (DJIA) from the early 1900s to the present. As you can see from the lines I have drawn, historically long periods exist when the DJIA index traded sideways, showing no gain and no loss. The most significant years were from 1929 to 1954. The market crashed in 1929, beginning the Great Depression. Notice that it took the market twenty-five years to recoup. Imagine if you had retired in 1929 and had all of your money invested in stocks. YIKES. Then you heard your broker say, "Don't worry Mr. and Mrs. Jones, the market goes up; it always does over a long period of time." Your time horizon isn't getting longer as you get older. It is getting shorter, so it makes sense to reduce your exposure to the market's volatility as time marches on.

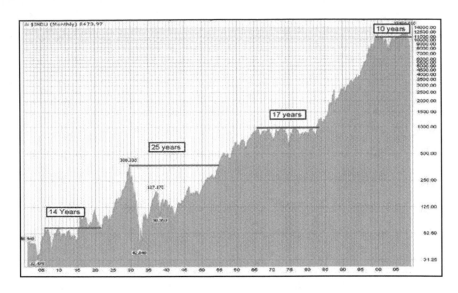

Not long ago, a prospective client came in for a second opinion on her investment portfolio. Her assets had nose-dived during 2008, and she had asked her broker to put her into a "safer" position. He moved her into bonds, which are not "safe" by my definition, but that wasn't the worst of it. She was eighty years old and could probably expect to live to be ninety. Since her broker had sold her twenty-year bonds, if she would need that money during her lifetime, she would have to cash in the bonds early and possibly sell them at a loss. If she died without needing the money, her beneficiaries would have to wait the additional years before they could liquidate the bonds without a loss. When I told this story to Jane Bryant Quinn, one of the nation's leading commentators on personal finance whom I interviewed on my radio show, her only comment was, "That man should be in jail."

You need to understand your own life expectancy. If you are in great health, exercise regularly, and have a family history of longevity, then you should plan to live a longer life. We have a few life expactancy calculators we recommend on the resources page on **www.soundretirementplanning.com**.

BONDS—WHAT KEEPS ME UP AT NIGHT

I hate to toot my own horn, but as you saw from the email I sent to our clients in 2008, I warned about our economy falling off a cliff very early on. They say hindsight is 20/20, and we can all look back now at the housing bubble and think, "I should have known it was coming." Of course, financial advisers all try to recognize trends early so they can position their clients before things get too ugly. When I shine up my crystal ball, here is what I see happening in the future.

Bonds are often touted as a safe alternative to stocks. Recent articles and evidence have suggested that bonds are safer than stocks over the long haul. However, bonds carry a substantial amount of risk and should not be discussed as safe. If you can lose money due to market volatility, then it is not safe.

Bonds have several different risks including default risk, credit risk, and call risk to name a few. I am going to discuss what I believe is the **most obvious risk of all right now—interest rate and term/maturity risk.** Bonds have a direct relationship with interest rates. If you buy a bond today, and it is paying an interest rate of 4 percent, but tomorrow the interest rates go up, so you could now buy a bond at 5 percent, then you could potentially lose money on the bond you purchased yesterday at 4 percent interest if you had to liquidate the bond before maturity.

Why would anyone want to buy a 4 percent bond from me when he could buy a bond from the issuer at 5 percent? Well, they won't want to buy your bond at 4 percent unless you discount the price. When you discount the price, it means you may receive less than your original investment back in return. If you hold a bond today and interest rates go up, your bond will be worth less money if you have to sell your bond before its maturity.

The question to ask is, "Are interest rates going to stay flat, go down, or go up in the future?" Take a look at a historical chart of the federal funds rate below before answering this question. The federal funds rate is the interest rate at which private depository institutions (mostly banks) lend balances (federal funds) at the Federal Reserve to other depository institutions, usually overnight. It is the interest rate banks charge each other for loans.

The U.S. Federal Government is printing money like crazy. Interest rates are at a historical all time low and likely go up.

In the early 1970s, the stock market crashed. The Dow Jones Industrial Average (DJIA) fell 45 percent. That was a doozie. Prior to the crash, the federal funds rate was at 12 percent. The federal funds rate is one way the Federal Reserve influences short-term interest rates and encourages economic growth. By lowering the rate, the Federal Reserve allowed for cheaper borrowing, which in turn should have stimulated the economy.

By 1976, the federal funds rate had plunged from 12 percent to less than 6 percent. Why is this important? How do people react after they lose 45 percent in a stock market sell off? They go to their broker and say, "Mr. Broker, I want more safety." So the

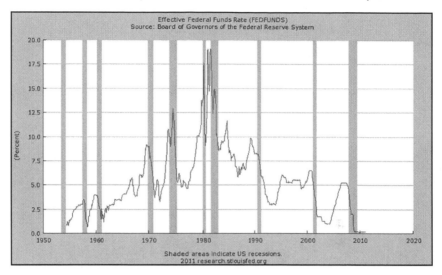

broker, following the common wisdom that bonds are safer than stocks, rebalances the client's portfolio and puts more money in bonds and less in stocks.

But by 1981, the federal funds rate had skyrocketed to 18 percent. So even though you were buying bonds for more safety in 1976, you were buying in at 6 percent or less. A few years later, you could buy bonds that were paying 18 percent or more. If you had to liquidate your 6 percent bonds before maturity, you would have taken a great big bath. And if you didn't liquidate the bonds, you saw all of your friends earning three times the yield. Bonds are not as safe as you might think.

Fast forward to 2007. The federal funds rate in 2007 was 4 percent before the market crashed, and as of April 2018, it's at 1.5 percent. People are going to their brokers and saying, "I want more safety."

You can see where this is going. The broker rebalances the client's portfolio to a stronger bond position and ... .Well, the future has yet to happen, but folks, if I were a betting man, I'd have to bet interest rates are going to be higher in the future. Remember, if interest rates go up and you hold a bond, the value of your bond is likely to go down. You could recognize a loss if you had to liquidate that bond before maturity.

One of the primary reasons I believe interest rates are going to go up is because of the political stalemate in our country. We have recently experienced Government shutdowns. We need foreign nations to finance all of the spending we are doing. These countries are not very excited about buying a 30-year treasury bond that is paying three percent when our dollar is down the tubes and losing ground as we continue to print money. The solution: The U.S. will have to raise interest rates to continue to attract capital from our foreign financiers.

So what can you do about it? If you are looking for a more conservative portfolio, then you must use other money alternatives that are guaranteed, and where you always know your worst case scenario.

We can use bonds as a negatively correlated asset class to stocks to help offset your portfolio for your at-risk and market sensitive investments, but bonds are not guaranteed either. Always remember to ask about the term of the bond. If you are retired and are seventy years old, do you really want to buy a twenty-year bond?

Don't fool yourself about the strength of the company in which you are investing. Things change. What you may perceive as a strong company today may not look too good in just a few years. Just look at Chrysler, Lehman Brothers, Enron, GM, Worldcom, Bear Stearns, and Washington Mutual.

Just remember you can lose money in bonds, so they should be used with caution and should be considered an at-risk investment rather than a guaranteed one.

Two very important terms you should familiarize yourself with if you are going to invest in bond mutual funds are:

- Average Effective Duration

- Average Effective Term/Maturity

Average effective duration essentially measures interest rate sensitivity. The longer the duration, the more volatility you can expect. A portfolio that has an average duration of twenty years would be twice as volatile as a portfolio with an average duration of ten years.

Average effective maturity measures the weighted average of all the maturities within the portfolio.

It is critical that you know and understand both of these numbers. If you currently hold bond mutual funds, please contact a financial adviser who will run reports to help you uncover and decipher this information.

Why do we diversify among stocks and bonds? Stocks provide for potential growth, and our hope and goal for growth is generally greater than inflation. We are willing to take risk with stocks because our hope is to outpace inflation over a long period of time, and stocks have a the potential for helping to accomplish that.

Bonds, on the other hand, are usually purchased to smooth volatility in a stock portfolio and generate income.

THE COST OF KEEPING SHORT TERM CDS

If you had money available to earn interest, then which would you rather have?

- $84 of interest in one year?

- Or $797 of interest in one year?

That is a big difference in the amount of interest after just one year, and I'm going to share with you exactly how and why you might want to consider an alternate vehicle for your money.

We recently had a client contact me and she said, "Jason I have a CD at the credit union that is about to mature." She went on to say, "Last year I earned about $75 of interest on $29,000. The CD is going to rollover soon, and the new rate is only going to be 0.29 percent."

Yes … you read that correctly.

She will earn a little more than ¼ of one percent if she leaves her money at the credit union. We've found some people mistakenly move the decimal point and think they are earning 2.9 percent. Not in this case. She would in fact be earning only 0.29 percent for a one year certificate of deposit. This is why some people now say "CD" stands for certificate of disappointment.

	Rates Constant for 5 years				
1	$100,000.00	2.75%		$2,750.00	$102,750.00
2	$102,750.00	2.75%		$2,825.63	$105,575.63
3	$105,575.63	2.75%		$2,903.33	$108,478.95
4	$108,478.95	2.75%		$2,983.17	$111,462.13
5	$111,462.13	2.75%		$3,065.21	$114,527.33
	Rates Rising at .25% per year				
1	$100,000.00	0.50%		$500.00	$100,500.00
2	$100,500.00	0.75%		$753.75	$101,253.75
3	$101,253.75	1.00%		$1,012.54	$102,266.29
4	$102,266.29	1.25%		$1,278.33	$103,544.62
5	$103,544.62	1.50%		$1,553.17	$105,097.79
	Rates Rising at .50% per year				
1	$100,000.00	0.50%		$500.00	$100,500.00
2	$100,500.00	1.00%		$1,005.00	$101,505.00
3	$101,505.00	1.50%		$1,522.58	$103,027.58
4	$103,027.58	2.00%		$2,060.55	$105,088.13
5	$105,088.13	2.50%		$2,627.20	$107,715.33
	Rates Rising at 1% per year				
1	$100,000.00	0.50%		$500.00	$100,500.00
2	$100,500.00	1.50%		$1,507.50	$102,007.50
3	$102,007.50	2.50%		$2,550.19	$104,557.69
4	$104,557.69	3.50%		$3,659.52	$108,217.21
5	$108,217.21	4.50%		$4,869.77	$113,086.98

When it comes to principal preservation, in order to get a higher fixed interest rate, you generally have to commit to a longer period of time. For this client, she was instead able to find a fixed deferred insurance contract that guaranteed 2.75 percent interest if she would commit to a five year term. In the historic context of interest rates, 2.75 percent does not sound very good. But if she earns 2.75 percent interest on $29,000 the first year, then she will earn $797 of interest. If she sticks with the CD she would earn about $84 in interest. Given the options she has available today, I'd say the choice is pretty straight forward.

But what if you commit to five years and then interest rates go up before the 5 year maturity?

Many people don't like the idea of committing to a five year period of time in a low interest rate environment, but there may be a cost to keeping short term CDs. I created a quick spreadsheet (see previous page) to try and determine the cost of keeping the CD's short term assuming the CD is rolled over every year and every year interest rates are going up.

You can see the results. I assumed a couple of different scenarios with interest rates rising: 0.25 percent, 0.50 percent, and 1 percent every year for the next 5 years. I've highlighted what the value of her account will be at the end of five years given the different scenarios. Obviously there is a cost of waiting.

WORLDS OF MONEY

Imagine you are seventy years old with a comfortable retirement and a $1 million nest egg. You are drawing $40,000 per year to supplement your retirement pension and Social Security income. Everything is going great, and your financial adviser says all is well since your withdrawal rate is at only about 4 percent; according to most financial professionals, that is a safe level of withdrawal at which you would not risk depleting your life savings.

You have followed your financial adviser's recommendation and diversified your investments among stocks, bonds, mutual funds, and ETFs. Then 2008 hits and suddenly you face one of the worst recessions since the Great Depression. In one year, you watch your life savings drop from $1 million to $500,000. Your financial adviser calls you into his office and explains that you are now draining your portfolio at 8 percent per year, and at that rate a much higher possibility exists that you will run out of money before you reach the end of your life.

You then have to choose between two frightening options: Would you like to cut your retirement income in half? Or risk running out of money? Frankly, we don't like either of these options and neither should you.

Understanding the different financial worlds you can use to diversify your investment assets is important in building your investment strategy for retirement. Many advisers hunker down under one investment philosophy, and they refuse to look at the alternatives that exist.

The plans we help people create isn't about me or my team. It's about helping our clients find ways to achieving their goals, dreams, and aspirations, and doing so with confidence in a retirement plan. To give them that confidence, we have to be flexible in our thinking and evaluate opportunities as they show up.

In my firm, we recommend our clients diversify across three different money worlds: **Principal Preservation, Equity-linked accounts, and Growth.**

THE WORLD OF PRINCIPAL PRESERVATION

Three institutions make up this world of principal preservation: banks, governments, and insurance companies. If you go to a bank and say, "Mr. Banker, I want my money guaranteed and earning the highest rate of return," the banker will recommend CDs. The government will offer U.S. Savings bonds, and insurance companies will offer deferred fixed annuities. All three financial vehicles share common characteristics. First, your principal is protected from loss. Second, you earn a fixed rate of interest. And finally, if you want to draw your money out of these accounts before the end of the term, you will pay a penalty/surrender charge for early withdrawal. These options are considered fairly conservative and do not typically offer high interest rates for your money.

THE WORLD OF GROWTH

Three institutions participate in the growth world: mutual fund companies, brokerage firms, and insurance companies. If you go to a mutual fund company and say, "Mr. Mutual Fund, I want my money to outpace inflation," a mutual fund company is going to recommend a mutual fund from its company. If you call up Vanguard for example, its advisers will likely recommend a Vanguard mutual fund.

Brokerage firms will offer a variety of investment tools that are large and growing: stocks, bonds, mutual funds, ETFs, REITS, limited partnerships, commodities, hedge funds, and the list goes on. Insurance companies will offer variable annuities.

Insurance companies work in both the growth and principal preservation worlds. On the principal preservation side of the equation, they offer fixed annuities and on the growth side variable annuities. A variable annuity is an investment in which your funds are pooled together with others and invested in underlying mutual funds.

Growth world investments share a couple of characteristics. First, your principal is not guaranteed and you could lose money. Second, you will earn a variable rate of return, and finally, if you really want to take advantage of the world of growth, you need TIME on your side.

When you are investing in the world of growth, you need to understand the historical volatility of the stock market. Look at a chart of the S&P 500 on a daily basis. You see very sharp peaks and valleys. Wild swings in market volatility, on a short-term basis, are expected. If you stand back and look at a chart of the S&P 500 during a fifteen-year time horizon, you will notice the volatility is much less extreme. Ultimately, TIME is the cure to volatility in the stock market. The more time you have on your side, the more volatility your investment portfolio can handle.

Earlier in this book, I discussed your time horizon versus the market's time horizon. If you are seventy-five years old and your life expectancy is eighty-four, you may not have enough time to participate in the world of growth.

The term growth is used interchangeably with the words equity, stocks, and risk throughout this book.

THE WORLD OF EQUITY-LINKED ACCOUNTS

In the mid-1990s, insurance companies began to develop products to fit the space between CDs and mutual funds. Banks and brokerage companies quickly hopped on board the bandwagon by creating their own equity-linked accounts.

Insurance companies developed a new breed of annuities with the Fixed Index Annuity (FIA), which provides: protection of your principal, a guaranteed minimum interest rate (usually 0-1 percent) with surrender charges for early withdrawal, and the potential to earn interest that's tied to the performance of an external market index such as the S&P 500. This annuity offers a guaranteed lifetime income stream, but also the potential for greater accumulation. The annuity is still a fixed insurance product, and you are never invested in the market. In addition, companies set limits on how much interest you can earn using caps, spreads and participation rates. For example, if you purchased an FIA with a 6 percent cap and the market index you chose soared to 14 percent in one year, then you would be limited to 6 percent interest and not the full 14 percent. (This scenario assumes you are using what's called the point-to-point crediting method with a cap). These contracts offer a number of crediting strategies, and they are designed to work in different market conditions, which means that no one strategy is best in every situation.

You're probably thinking, "Well, that's crummy. I want to earn the 14 percent." But remember, you also can't lose anything on a down year due to market loss (although surrender charges for early withdrawals could reduce your principal amount). So if the stock market goes down the next year, you stay at 0 percent growth and 0 percent loss.

Let's assume you have an FIA with an 6 percent cap linked to the S&P 500, and during the course of one year, the S&P 500 increased by 10 percent; then your index annuity would credit you with an 6 percent interest rate for the year. The great thing about that 6 percent interest is that it is now locked in, and you can't lose that interest based on future stock market performance. So if you purchased an FIA with $100,000 and earned 6% interest based on the external market changes on your first contract anniversary, your annuity value would be $106,000. (Keep in mind that your actual amount available for withdrawal will be less due to surrender charge in the contract's early years.)

But the real power of the index annuity is displayed in years when the stock market declines. For example, let's say in the second year of the contract, the S&P 500 fell by 10 percent. Remember, your annuity has grown to $106,000. In a year when the market declines by 10 percent, you don't lose a penny due to market loss. You don't make anything in that year, but you don't lose either. These FIAs can be a great tool to help you fight inflation. Insurance companies offer Fixed Indexed Annuities. Banks offer equity linked CDs and brokerage companies offer indexed notes.

All these vehicles are designed to protect your principal while giving you the opportunity to earn a rate of return greater than you might earn in a traditional fixed rate account. Of the three available, I often recommend a fixed index annuity for retirees because of the guarantees and lifetime income they offer.

In a study by Jack Marrion, Geoffrey VanderPal, and David Babbel from Wharton School of business[11], they argued that these FIAs have performed favorably during the past ten years. Granted, the last ten years the stock market has had a bad run. But that's precisely why these tools were created. Because we can't begin to guess what the stock market will do, the FIA is a way to earn interest that involves some upside exposure to the market while protecting principal.

Roger Ibbotson, who is a professor emeritus at Yale school of school of management and a 10 time recipient of Graham & Dodd Awards for financial research excellence, and his team at Zebra Capital Management recently published a white paper titled *Fixed Indexed Annuities: Consider the Alternative.*[12]

11 Marrion, Jack et al. Wharton Financial Institutions Center Personal Finance: Real World Index Annuity Returns. October, 5 2009. http://www.nafa.com/resources/nafa-file-archives/2009/doc_download/613-2009-wfic-real-world-index-annuity-returns.html. Accessed February 25, 2011

12 https://www.prnewswire.com/news-releases/renowned-economist-roger-ibbotson-unveils-new-research-indicating-fixed-indexed-annuities-may-outperform-bonds-

Today, Ibbotson's latest research suggests that an FIA (uncapped and subject to a spread) helps control equity market risk and mitigate longevity risk.

"Conventional wisdom has most investors de-risking their portfolios by allocating more heavily to bonds as they approach retirement," continued Ibbotson. "However, investors should consider other alternatives such as FIAs. In this low interest rate environment, complacency can be a danger to our clients' futures."

FIAs can be an alternative or complement to traditional fixed income/principal preservation vehicles such as CDs or government bonds, but they are likely not a viable replacement for the funds you have in the market for equity/growth positions, depending on your risk tolerance and personal situation. As of this writing, the U.S. Federal Government has set the federal funds rate at essentially 1.5 percent. When interest rates begin to climb, bond holders could see a significant loss if they have to liquidate their bonds before maturity. But with an FIA, you always know the worst case position if you have to exit your contract early, whereas, with bonds you have more unknowns and more volatility.

HOW MUCH RISK SHOULD YOU TAKE?

Let's take a look at how you can use the tools within each of these different worlds to create a plan to provide you with a good balance of principal preservation and growth so you can protect

over-the-next-decade-300609670.html

your assets from stock market risk and still help protect your assets from inflation risk.

Many advisers use the Age-100 rule of thumb to determine how much of your investment portfolio should be invested in risk positions versus how much should be invested in principal preservation positions. It's a simple equation and may not be an appropriate mix depending on the purpose of your money. You may need to be more or less aggressive to ensure you don't run out of money. But let's use the rule of Age-100 as a starting point.

Take your current age and subtract it from 100. Let's say you are sixty, so if you subtract that from 100, it equals forty. According to the Age-100 rule, you would want 40 percent of your liquid assets invested in growth/risk position (a position that battles inflation but where you can also lose money), and 60 percent in a principal preservation position (a position that protects your principal from stock market risk, but may not keep pace with inflation).

The closer you get to age 100, the more money you want in principal preservation positions since you are transitioning through retirement and are running out of time. Remember, time is the ultimate cure for the volatility of your growth/risk accounts. As you get older, it becomes more important to protect against market risk than it does to protect against inflation risk.

While stock market volatility can erode your principal overnight, inflation is usually a slow moving train that eats away at your buying power over time. Both risks are real and important, but

I want to make sure you diversify appropriately given your time horizon rather than the market's time horizon.

Run this calculation for yourself. Then take a look at your investments to see whether they match up with this rule for diversifying. Many people will find the majority of their money is still in a growth position. We see many people with 70 to 90 percent of their retirement assets invested in growth vehicles. Many portfolios generally have a mix of stocks, bonds, mutual funds, and a little cash, and those folks assume they have a properly diversified portfolio. Not understanding what makes up a properly diversified portfolio is one of the biggest mistakes many retirees make.

You will notice that stocks and bonds are vehicles that are both situated in the world of growth, which is fine when you are younger, have time on your side, or are in an upward trending market. But in a year like 2008, where treasuries were the only asset class not losing money, focusing solely on growth is a crummy strategy. It's not uncommon for me to hear stories about people who lost 30 percent or more of their retirement savings by having most of their money in growth positions.

DON'T PUT ALL YOUR EGGS IN ONE BASKET

Recently, I was watching a TV program where the host was discussing investing and taking telephone calls from viewers. A man called and said, "I have three stocks, they are blank, blank, and blank. Am I diversified? The host said, "Um, let's see. You have energy, entertainment, and medical," or something like that and then said, "Boy, that is GREAT. That is one of the best diversified portfolios I have seen."

That isn't a direct quote, but the situation was close enough to that. Now if I were investing our clients' retirement life savings using this model of diversification, I wouldn't sleep very well at night. Unfortunately, when I meet with many people for the first time, they tell me, "Oh yes, I'm diversified. My adviser told me I am." Then I start to dig around a little and find they aren't diversified at all.

When I was a boy, my dad used to say that diversification means not putting all of your eggs in one basket. I have carried that advice with me, and I now use a strategy to help ensure our clients don't have all of their eggs in one basket or in this case investment worlds.

Some clients believe they are diversified because they are following the age-100 rule so at age sixty they have $100,000 with $60,000 in bonds and $40,000 in an stock mutual fund. Can you lose money in bonds? If you had money invested in bonds in 2008, you know you can. We even saw some people lose money in the money market accounts in the great crash of 2008. So if you can lose money in bonds would that qualify as a safe place? NO. NO. NO. **A growth position, in my definition, is any investment where you can lose money**. Some people only refer to stocks as growth, but we also refer to bonds as growth because you can lose money. Many people own mutual funds, but they don't know what each of those mutual funds is invested in. So according to the example above, they have all $100,000 in risk vehicles where they can lose money.

Remember, you're retired now. You're not contributing anything more to the nest egg you have accumulated. What you have is what you have, and it may need to last a very long time in retirement. Be cautious, if your adviser talks to you about diversification, and you have a large percentage invested in bonds and mutual funds, then it may be time for a second opinion.

DIVERSIFYING YOUR TIME HORIZON AND INVESTMENT SELECTION

Don't bring a knife to a gun fight.
— Author Unknown

We frequently find people who have a brokerage account with a mix of stocks and bonds and are following the Age-100 rule. We've already discussed why we don't believe bonds are risk-free, so let's assume these people, at my advice, have moved their accounts from bonds

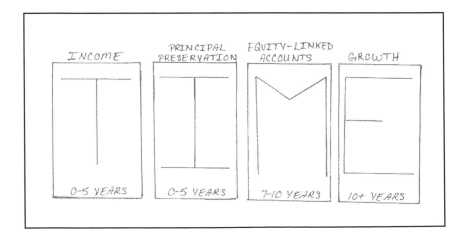

to truly "principal preservation" tools, but we don't believe they should stop there. We believe they should take their diversification strategy one step further.

Instead of just diversifying across growth and principal preservation accounts, you should also diversify your time horizon. This strategy is especially important for retirees who need their savings to supplement their incomes. By diversifying your time horizon, you are allocating your assets across multiple segments with each segment having a specific goal. If you were building a deck and wanted to screw the decking down, you wouldn't use a hammer to do the job. The same is true with each segment of your retirement strategy. What you want to do is to use the best tool for the job at hand.

Let's say you are sixty years old and you plan on living to age ninety. You could diversify your money across three time segments. Each segment would have a specific goal. Essentially, this diversification strategy is designed to buy time. (Diversification and asset allocation do not ensure a profit or guarantee against losses.)

The first segment will be your least risky and might have a five-year time horizon associated with it. This segment is the money you plan to use for immediate income needs so you cannot take any risk at all with these assets. You are likely looking at choices such as laddering CDs, using money market accounts, or single premium immediate annuities. Your ultimate goal for the first segment is preservation of principal, and your second objective is return.

Your next segment is constructed for years five to ten. Because you have a little more time on your side, you can probably afford to take a little more risk depending on your personal risk tolerance. But you still want a high degree of principal preservation for this second stage because you know that at the end of the first five years, you are going to need to rely on these investments to continue to provide for income. But again, you are buying time. Because you know you won't need this money for five years, you can afford to take more risks. You are less concerned with liquidity. You can ladder five-year CDs, or consider fixed annuities, or if you are willing to take a little more risk, you can buy highly rated individual corporate bonds or government bonds with a five-year maturity. You would continue to construct a retirement plan using multiple segments with each segment using the best tool for its specific purpose.

By the time you are at the third segment, you know you will have a 10 to 15 year time horizon. With this money, you can afford to take the most risk because you know you won't have to touch these assets for 10 years.

DIVERSIFYING WITHIN YOUR GROWTH WORLD: THE ART AND SCIENCE OF INVESTING

We've talked about diversifying or laddering your investments across the three different worlds of: principal preservation, multiple-use products, and growth, and across your time horizon, but you also want to diversify within your growth accounts. For our clients' equity positions, we recommend two methodologies for diversifying their growth assets, one of which won the Nobel

Prize in economics. When my team tells our clients their equity positions are diversified, we have a time-tested method we use for monitoring and comparing their portfolios. We constantly monitor the asset allocation and the money managers and make adjustments any time our clients' portfolios fall outside of their desired asset allocation. This style of institutional money management is newly available to the average investor. One of the reasons I started Parker Financial is because I believe every investor should have access to these tools.

I subscribe to two different philosophies that can be combined for how you can invest your money in the stock market:

- Tactical Investment Management — The Art of Investing

- Strategic Asset Allocation — The Science of Investing

We'll take a look at each of these below. I recognize that some people will believe strongly about one or the other investment style so much so that they will be unwilling to bend or see investing from the other perspective. For some, it's all or nothing. But I believe both of these styles are justifiable for different reasons. I tell our clients both are good investment styles, and depending on market conditions, different strategies may perform better than others.

When it comes to our clients' retirement savings and retirement plans working, I'd rather be right 50 percent of the time than wrong 100 percent of the time. With the current extreme volatility we are seeing in the market, I am recommending that clients consider using both strategic and tactical investments as appropriate.

Depending on a client's risk tolerance, goals and objectives, I typically recommend having 30 percent allocated toward a tactical (art) hands-on approach and 70 percent allocated to a strategic (scientific) indexing approach.

TACTICAL INVESTMENT MANAGEMENT

In tactical investment management, the managers are seeking opportunities and looking to avoid risk by actively trading and managing a portfolio, which means they will, at times, move your investments out of the stock market. This style of management is the "art" side of investing. It can't be academically or scientifically proven, but some managers have had very impressive results over a long period of time. Even though no guarantees exist that these results will continue into the future, you would be hard-pressed to discount what some of the tactical money managers have achieved.

STRATEGIC ASSET ALLOCATION

Strategic asset allocation was born through Modern Portfolio Theory (MPT). Harry Markowitz and William F. Sharpe won the Nobel Prize in 1990 for developing this theory. In October 2013, Eugene Fama won the Nobel Prize for Efficient Market Hypothesis (EMH), which is often associated with MPT. EMH asserts financial markets are informationally efficient and one cannot consistently predict returns in excess of the average Market returns.

MPT proposes how rational investors will use diversification to optimize their portfolios, and how a risk asset should be priced. MPT assumes that investors are risk averse, meaning that given two assets that offer the same expected return, investors will prefer the less risky one. Thus, an investor will take on increased risk only if compensated by higher expected returns. Conversely, an investor who wants higher returns must accept more risk.

The exact trade-off will differ by investor, based upon individual risk aversion characteristics. The implication is that a rational investor will not invest in a portfolio if a second portfolio exists with a more favorable risk-return profile—i.e., if for that level of risk an alternative portfolio exists, which has better expected returns, the rational investor will choose it. A landmark study conducted in 1991 and expanded in 1993 suggests that portfolio asset allocation is the most important long-term determinant of investment results. Strategic asset allocation also suggests that no one can accurately and consistently predict when shifts in market leadership will occur or how long they will last. The market leaders of one year often become the laggards the next.

Strategic asset allocation, therefore, suggests that it's important to spread your assets across multiple investment asset classes and sectors so you can potentially benefit from an upswing in any one asset class. It also suggests that the stock market is efficient and that all asset classes do not move in tandem. So the hope is that when one asset class zigs, the other zags, because we are looking for balance between these asset classes. In 2008 when the market went haywire, this type of strategy didn't work very well. The only negatively correlated asset class was treasuries. Typically, when stocks drop, bonds increase. But because of the fear in 2008, even high quality bond mutual funds lost money. Many of those bond funds made a strong recovery once people got their senses back and fear resided.

THE SECRET TO BUYING LOW AND SELLING HIGH

Have you ever heard that the secret to success in the stock market is to "buy low and sell high?" Unfortunately, many studies point out that individual investors are fairly bad at timing the stock market. These studies suggest that most people tend to invest after a long and sustained bull market, and then they sell after the market has crashed. Essentially they are buying high and selling low.What if a way existed to strategically buy low and sell high? Would you want to know about it? And when would you plan to implement it?

One of the ways I believe you can intelligently invest in the stock market is to create a broadly diversified portfolio across asset classes and sectors diversified across the entire globe. This method of diversification is what I call strategic asset allocation and is built by using low-cost index mutual funds or exchange traded funds (ETFs). The powerful ingredient that really makes strategic asset allocation work is re-balancing the portfolio. Re-balancing is counter-intuitive because it forces you to sell some of your winners and buy more of your losers. But if you believe that the market is efficient, then you believe that no one asset class or sector will ever dominate from year-to-year and that eventually a regression in the mean will happen. So while large-cap growth may be the best asset class this year, perhaps small-cap value will be the best next year, and treasury-inflation-protected securities the next.

Re-balancing is an intelligent way to buy low and sell high. How often should you re-balance your portfolio can and should be debated. Some people will re-balance a portfolio based on a calendar year of historical data. An old saying goes, "Sell in May and go away." But instead of selling, some will use this historical data to re-balance their portfolio in May instead. Depending on whether you have your money invested in a qualified or non-qualified account may impact how often you want to re-balance your portfolio from a tax-planning standpoint.

We set the drift parameters for our strategic portfolios at anywhere from 2 percent to 3 percent. So anytime one asset class has drifted out of alignment by more than 2 percent or 3 percent, that is an indicator to us to re-balance a portfolio.

In summary, one way to make money in the stock market is to buy low and sell high. Re-balancing a portfolio that is broadly diversified across asset classes and sectors across the entire globe is a strategic, non-emotional way of helping you do just that.

Many academic articles have been written on Modern Portfolio Theory (MPT), Efficient Market Hypothesis (EMH), and the benefits of strategic asset allocation. Many of the greatest minds in finance recognize these theories and many will argue that they are the only way to invest your money. They have proven track records and are used by many large institutions for managing billions of dollars.

Both strategic and tactical investment styles offer advantages and disadvantages. Market conditions will determine which one of these two styles will perform the best. In an upward trending market like we had from the early 1980s to 1999, strategic asset allocation will probably perform best. In a very volatile market like we had in 2008, tactical asset allocation has performed better. They are both good, and as we said, we'd rather be right 50 percent of the time than wrong 100 percent of the time.

WHY DIVIDENDS? WHY NOW?

Since the early 1930s, dividends have accounted for more than 40 percent of the total return of large-cap stocks in the United States.[13]

As baby boomers begin to transition into and through retirement, they're going to be looking for ways to generate income from their investments while, at the same time, trying to keep pace with inflation. The fact that 10 thousand boomers are retiring every day is reason to give pause and pay attention to income-producing investments. Members of the baby boomer generation have several options to try to pursue their income and lifestyle goals. Below are a few of the most common:

- They can buy bonds and live off the income from the bonds.

---

13 https://www.hartfordfunds.com/dam/en/docs/pub/whitepapers/WP106.pdf
https://www.fidelity.com/insights/investing-ideas/7-best-mutual-funds-for-dividends
https://www.investopedia.com/ask/answers/042415/what-average-annual-return-sp-500.asp

- They can purchase dividend-paying stocks and live off of the income from the dividend paying stocks.

- They can purchase an annuity and have a guaranteed income stream from an insurance company.

- They can use a total return approach to portfolio management and retirement income by applying the 4 percent rule that says you shouldn't take out more than 4 percent per year from a properly diversified portfolio or you risk running out of money in retirement.

In light of the current economic conditions, slower global growth is reasonably expected and higher inflation is anticipated. Just how do we plan to cope with a rising interest rate environment.

Dividend-paying stocks have become very attractive because they tend to have favorable fundamental attributes and have historically exhibited lower levels of volatility. Creating a portfolio of diversified dividend-paying stocks that have a track record for dividend growth can help investors seeking income to create a hedge against inflation.

Dividend growth means you have the potential to receive more income next year than you received this year if the companies you invest in raise their dividends. This could help you maintain your lifestyle and income needs plus help you hedge inflation as you transition through retirement. Many companies have a long track record of paying and raising their dividends.

Bonds have a negative correlation to interest rates. So when interest rates eventually begin to rise the value of your bond portfolio would decline, and you could lose money if you had to sell your bond before the maturity date. When you hold bonds in mutual funds you lose out on the ability to hold individual bonds to maturity. Because the federal reserve has set short term interest rates at 1.5 percent. For this reason a forward-looking income investor would be wise to focus on individual bonds they are willing to hold to maturity and/or dividend paying stocks that are trading at fair valuations.

When considering a stock for dividend growth potential, one of the most important factors is the payout ratio. The payout ratio is basically the company's dividend per share divided by their net earnings per share. For example if the dividend is $2 and the net earnings per share is $4 you have a 50 percent payout ratio (2/4=0.50). Looking for stocks that have a long term track record of paying dividends, raising dividends and have a payout ratio of less than 50 percent could help an investor gauge whether the future of a dividend is likely to continue and if the company has potential to grow their dividends in years to come.

For many investors headed into retirement, a combination of all of the different income tools available will probably make sense to help them create a retirement plan that meets their need for income, inflation and protection in conjunction with their risk tolerance. Be sure to find an adviser that can help you explore all of your options and construct a plan that can help you achieve clarity, confidence and freedom.

Chapter 4

SAVING SAFELY IN RETIREMENT

Now that you know how important it is to focus on the future, not only for your own retirement, but so you can leave a legacy to your family, you need to learn how to make the money you have last throughout your retirement. The last thing you want to do is run out of money before you run out of life, and if you don't plan carefully, in today's economy, that scenario can become a very real possibility.

SENIORS ARE BEING SQUEEZED

Senior citizens are being squeezed, and I'm not talking about bear hugs from the grandkids. Higher property taxes along with inflation are driving up the costs of gasoline, food, healthcare, and insurance. Couple these with a very volatile stock market, longer life expectancies, and declining yields on fixed income investments, and we have an especially alarming trend for folks who are retired.

When people retire, they shift from a strategy of accumulating assets to a strategy of preserving and distributing the assets they have accumulated. Certificates of Deposit (CDs) seem to be a popular safe haven for many of these folks. While CDs certainly preserve principal another alternative does exist.

Hypothetically, if the overnight national average yield on a five-year CD is currently 3.24 percent and assuming these are taxable dollars, then you should calculate your yield after-tax. So if you are in the 25 percent marginal tax bracket, then the after-tax yield on your CD is only 2.43 percent. Then factor in a conservative estimate of 3 percent for inflation, and you can see inflation and taxes are taking a big bite out of your bottom line. Your principal is safe from market volatility, but not from taxes and inflation. For current rates visit **www.bankrate.com**.

A common tax planning strategy is to defer income from the current year to later years because a dollar in hand today is worth more than a dollar in the future: the time value of money. This concept is particularly important during inflationary times.

SAFETY—WHAT DOES IT MEAN TO YOU?

In my first meeting with prospective clients, I ask, "How much of your money do you want safe?" Most people have a hard time answering this question because they would like more safety, but still want to outpace inflation.

The root of this question is the word "safe." What does that word mean to you? It means different things to different people. At my firm, we often recommend putting some funds into the "principal preservation" bucket, which uses products where you won't lose your principal based on market fluctuations and can always calculate your worst case scenario when you need access to your money.

This really narrows the tools I will use to fill this segment of a retirement strategy.

Many people do not really understand bonds and think they will help offset market risk. Folks, bonds will not always work like you want them to if you don't know what the worst case future scenario will be if we have to liquidate the bond before maturity. This even applies to U.S. Treasury bonds. At least with a corporation, we have the ability to review their books to see whether they are worthy of an investment.

But the way our country is printing money and using quantitative easing, it's hard to determine whether U.S. Treasury bonds are a good deal. U.S. Treasury bonds are effective when held to maturity compared to any other bonds available, but if you have to liquidate your bond before maturity, it is possible to lose money on U.S. Treasury bonds depending on market conditions.

Let's take a quick minute to explore the three different vehicles that I believe are truly safe, secure and guaranteed.

- **Certificates of Deposit** are offered by banks and are commonly known as CDs. As long as you are working with a bank that is FDIC insured, and you are below the FDIC insurance limits, you will not lose any principal while invested in them.

- **Fixed Deferred Annuities** are offered by insurance companies. Similar to a CD, they pay a fixed rate of interest. Fixed deferred annuities are NOT FDIC insured.

Their guarantees are backed by the financial strength and claims-paying ability of the issuing company. The first line of defense is to make sure you are working with a highly rated insurance company. But if an insurance company should fail, most fixed annuities are guaranteed by your state's guarantee association. You can check how much of your principal is protected from loss by visiting **www.nolhga.com**.

- **U.S. Savings Bonds** are backed by the U.S. Government so if our country were to fail, you might lose your principal. If the U.S.A. fails, then your money probably won't be worth anything anyway. Unlike treasury bonds whose price will fluctuate with market conditions (interest rates), your savings bonds avoid that risk. One popular variation of the savings bond is the I Bond. The I Bond is a savings bond that pays interest, which is, in part, based on inflation. Unfortunately, how we calculate inflation these days is getting a little skewed. I can't understand why the cost of food and energy isn't included when determining inflation. Isn't that where most of us spend our money?

All three of these vehicles pay a fixed rate of interest. They have competitive rates. Generally speaking, CDs, fixed annuities, and savings bonds all carry a penalty if you withdraw your money before maturity. But you always know your worst case scenario if you have to liquidate the holding before maturity. And each involves its own unique guarantee or backing by the issuing entity. While all three products share some characteristics, they are distinctly different products designed for different purposes and are not automatically interchangeable.

Depending on whether you will be withdrawing the interest for income or just reinvesting the interest from your investments may have an impact on which of the above tools you use. For example, if you withdraw funds from an annuity, you could face surrender penalties depending on the contract.

Using CDs for non-qualified accounts has a disadvantage because you are taxed on your interest income even if you don't use it. That pesky 1099 will show up at the end of the year, and you will have to pay tax on your interest income.

Fixed deferred annuities and savings bonds both offer tax deferral, even in non-qualified accounts. So you control when you pay taxes. By controlling your tax liability, you have the opportunity to benefit from triple compounding: compounding on your interest, compounding on your principal, and compounding on your tax savings.

Obviously, the time value of money concept is applied here. The good folks at **www.investopedia.com** have this to say about it: "This core principal of finance holds that, provided money can earn interest, any amount of money is worth more the sooner it is received. This concept is also referred to as the present discount value."

The bottom line is: We want you to pay your fair share in taxes, but we want you to be in control of when you pay those taxes. We want you to be on the winning side of the "time value of money" concept and not the government.

Be sure to use a trusted third-party custodian for your investments, so you don't end up in a Bernie Madoff scam. (Bernie Madoff operated the largest Ponzi scheme in history. A Ponzi scheme is a fraudulent investment operation that pays returns to separate investors, not from any actual profit earned by the organization, but from their own money or money paid by subsequent investors.)

A custodian acts as the intermediary between you and your adviser. We currently work with Fidelity and Folio Institutional for our clients. Our clients' investment accounts are housed at these custodians. We have the ability to place trades in these accounts, but we cannot withdraw money from the accounts other than our fee for being their financial adviser. Only the client can access these accounts. This limited access provides an extra layer of protection for the client. Custodians mitigate the risk of dishonest activity by separating the fund managers from the physical securities and investor records.

STOCK MARKET VOLATILITY

2017 was an incredible year in the stock market and other than a few mid-year hiccups it only seemed to go up. As we ventured into 2018 we experienced a bit of a correction. Stock market volatility is on the rise and peoples sentiments quickly begin to change about their future when the markets begin to get wobbly.

I spoke with a friend this morning who said he and his wife were planning a river cruise through Europe. One of the reasons he chose to do this was because they are confident in their retirement plan.

Imagine a world where the stock market only went up. As nice as it sounds, that is just not the way the stock market has ever worked in the short term. Time is the only cure to the stock market volatility. The more time you have, then the more risk you can afford to take.

When you create your retirement plan being conservative is advisable especially for the income portion of that plan. When you take the conservative route to retirement income, you do not have to worry about the volatility of the stock market disrupting your cash flow or your lifestyle.

Diversify your portfolio so that time is on your side and when the markets get wobbly and fear begins to take root, you won't have to worry. Instead you can spend your mental energy planning your next adventure on a river cruise through Europe.

HOW SAFE IS YOUR RETIREMENT?

In 2016 you probably read in the news that Greece was on the verge of default and could possibly be leaving the Euro. At the same time, in 30 days, the Chinese Shanghai composite had lost over 30 percent, the Dow Jones Industrial Average was down -1 percent on the year, the Fed recently raised interest rates for the first time in seven years, and on top of all that, our debt in the United States had exceeded 19 trillion dollars.

When it comes to investing there is an old saying that "a rising tide lifts all boats," but Warren Buffet really nailed it when he said, "When the tide goes out you find out who has been swimming naked."

When it comes to retirement planning, we've seen too many people make the mistake of assuming a constant rate of return on their money (around 7-10 percent per year) without considering how the sequence of those returns can impact their retirement cash flow and investment portfolio. As I've said earlier, a significant loss the first couple of years of retirement could devastate a entire retirement withdrawal strategy. When it comes to retirement income it is not just the rate of return that matters, but the timing of those returns.

The solution to this problem is actually pretty simple: TIME. Time is the cure to the volatility of the stock market. The more time you have, the more risk you can afford to take. When you are drawing money out of a portfolio for retirement income, you want to make sure that income source is safe from market volatility. Taking money out of an account that is falling in value is like donating blood when you have been stabbed and are bleeding. You have a bad situation that is going to get worse.

Diversification of your portfolio in retirement should include two steps: **Step one** is to diversify your time horizon; **Step two** is to diversify your investments. Some people call this a bucket approach to retirement income while others refer to it as laddering your cash flow. Essentially income you need for the first five years falls under principal preservation. The more time you have, then the more risk you can afford to take. If you create a retirement income plan that diversifies time first and then uses the right financial vehicle for that time segment, then you can create a retirement income plan that is designed delivers greater confidence.

The key is to start with a plan, not an investment strategy. It is important that you stick with the plan in the good times and the bad. Unfortunately too many people make projections based on the good times. When the market is going up and the tide is rising, everyone is comfortable with risk. When the tide is going out and people begin to realize their plan is very vulnerable to the whims of the market, those who do not have a good retirement income strategy can begin making emotional decisions, which are usually bad decisions. The best time to buy something is when it is on sale. The best time to sell something is when it is at its peak price. When you do not have a good retirement cash flow plan to start with, many people end up making the exact opposite decisions. They sell assets when they are on sale, and they buy them when they are expensive.

Stock market volatility is nothing new. It has always been with us, and it will always be with us. It is the risk that we are willing to assume that allows us to have the potential to earn a return greater than we might get in a bank certificate of deposit.

When you have diversified your retirement income plan by time and conservatively solved for your cash flow needs, then you won't have to worry about people seeing you naked when the tide is going out.

BANKS AND FINANCIAL RATINGS

IndyMac Bank was seized by federal regulators in what was called, "The second largest bank failure in U.S. history." Thank goodness the FDIC exists to help protect deposits. With all of the turmoil in the financial sector, my clients want to know about the financial strength of their banks. According to the FDIC website:

The FDIC never releases its ratings on the safety and soundness of banks and thrift institutions to the public. As a service to consumers, the staff of the FDIC Library has compiled a listing of several financial institution rating services. ***Disclaimer:*** This list should not be construed as an endorsement or confirmation by the FDIC of information provided by these companies.

I clicked on several of the different rating agencies listed by the FDIC. The one I found easiest to navigate was offered by Bauer Financial at **www.bauerfinancial.com**. It offers a free rating report for banks and credit unions. And to keep the legal beagles happy, I will restate the following disclaimer: ***Parker Financial LLC does not endorse or confirm the information provided by Bauer Financial.***

When a bank fails, you will hear stories about people whose money was not covered by FDIC insurance because they were over the limits. Go to **www.fdic.gov** to review the FDIC's frequently asked questions, which should help clarify what is and is not covered by FDIC.

KEY RATING RESOURCES

- Visit AM Best at **www.ambest.com** to check on the financial strength of the insurance company offering your annuity.

- Visit Treasury Direct at **www.treasurydirect.gov** for buying your U.S. Savings bonds and I Bonds.

- Visit Bauer Financial at **www.bauerfinancial.com** to check on the financial strength of your bank.

- For a complete listing of the links and resources found in my book, please visit **www.soundretirementplanning.com**

IRRATIONAL EXUBERANCE

Robert Shiller is an American Nobel Prize winning economist and professor of economics at Yale University. According to his Wikipedia profile he is ranked among the 100 most influential economists in the world. I was recently reading the second edition of his book *Irrational Exuberance* when I read the following on page 222, under the heading, "Retirement Plans Should Be Put on a Sounder Footing." He writes:

> "Authorities who are responsible for pension plans (including agencies like the Pension Benefit Guarantee Corporation in the United States or the Pension Protection fund in the United Kingdom) should come out strongly against over-reliance on the stock market. They should instead recommend greater diversification and suggest that a substantial fraction of balances be put into safe investments, such as inflation indexed government bonds. They should promote inflation-indexed retirement annuities and urge retirees to take the retirement income in this form."

In a future chapter, I'll describe how ultra-conservative retirees can create an income stream by laddering annuities and adjusting their income for inflation. Of course, I wrote my book after Robert Shiller wrote *Irrational Exuberance*, but it sure is validating when one of the top economists in the world writes that our government should urge the use of inflation-indexed retirement annuities.

RETIREMENT FOR THE SELF-EMPLOYED

We have had the wonderful opportunity to work with many people who are retired business owners. Entrepreneurs tend to be cautiously optimistic and are very savvy. They have done a great job of building their businesses, making money, and adding value to people's lives. Oftentimes, though, they have not had the time nor inclination to really dive into personal finance. They just make it, save it, and keep working harder and harder. Then one day they realize they don't want to work forever.

One of the questions we often ask in our first meeting is, "If you could wave a magic wand and accomplish just one thing by us meeting today, what would it be?" The common reply usually has something to do with the words clarity and confidence. Sometimes I'll get the good humored reply of, "I want to earn 20 percent per year."

What entrepreneurs really want when it comes to their financial lives is an objective and honest assessment of where they stand. They want to know if the numbers will work. They want a plan that gives them clarity, so they can have the confidence to retire without having to worry, and they can experience the freedom they have worked hard for. What they do not want is a financial adviser who is out to sell them a financial product.

Entrepreneurs are looking for answers to questions and solutions to problems. Entrepreneurs understand the concept of cash flow better than most people because they know they can have all the assets in the world, but, at the end of the day, if they don't have cash and income they may find themselves in trouble because banks lend on income, not assets. The last thing they want to do is find themselves in a position where they are having to sell assets at a discount in order to come up with cash to keep operations going.

If you think this is unsettling as a business owner, then try doing this as a person struggling with the same cash flow concept in retirement. When you are working, you can make mistakes and recover. Once you have retired, you have less time to recover from a significant error.

Ultimately the two primary concerns most small business owners have as they begin to think about retirement are: How will we pay for health care? And have we saved enough money to provide cash flow to maintain our standard of living for a very long time?

In September 2017, Fidelity Benefits Consulting estimated that a couple who retires at age 65 is estimated to need $275,000 to cover medical expenses through retirement. This figure does not include any costs associated with nursing home care.[1]

I sometimes joke that the best retirement plan is to run for Congress because, according to Wikipedia, our elected leaders become vested for a pension after five years of service. What I think many of us find really attractive about a pension is the idea of the guaranteed income that it provides. As an entrepreneur, once you have retired, what you have is what you have and chances are

---

1   https://www.fidelity.com/viewpoints/retirement/retiree-health-costs-rise

you probably do not want to go back to work if the stock market performs poorly or interest rates rise rapidly.

Most of the people we serve don't seem interested in running for public office in order to secure a pension. (Although we have a feeling many of the people we serve would do an outstanding job if they did run for public office.) As an entrepreneur you might want to consider creating your own income retirement plan to solve for your cash flow needs.

One way to build this income strategy might be to ladder single premium and fixed deferred annuity contracts to create a guaranteed cash flow.

The emphasis when creating this type of plan is to solve for cash flow so that you do not have to worry about stock and bond market volatility when providing for your retirement income needs. When you consider mortality risk and treat it as an asset class, you can make some calculated estimates to shift the burden of lifetime income from a "what if" to a "guarantee" that the insurance companies can provide.

An annuity contract is the only way we can use the word "guarantee" when talking about future income. The key to making this work is for you to get into the insurance companies pockets as quickly as possible and then live a really long time. Insurance companies' are pretty darn good at looking at large groups of people to understand life expectancy risk, but they generally do not look at each individual's life expectancy. If you are in good health and have a history of longevity in your family, then you might want to consider this type of strategy.

Once you have an inflation-adjusted retirement cash flow, you may be able to take on more market risk without having to worry about a market correction disrupting your lifestyle.

As much as we all hate paying for insurance, I think we all hate paying the consequences of not having the right insurance even more.

Obviously many solutions exist for retirement income, but for those entrepreneurs who understand cash flow and its importance, then creating an income retirement plan can help you accomplish this goal.

Sometimes because entrepreneurs tend to be cautiously optimistic, they take on more risk than is necessary to accomplish their goals. You've worked too hard, accomplished too much, and have too much at stake to make a financial mistake at this point in your financial life. Remember, "A bird in the hand is better than two in the bush."

There are few financial vehicles that cause as much controversy as annuities. On one hand you have investment advisers who say they "hate annuities" One prominent investment advisor went as far as saying "I would die and go to hell before selling an annuity". That person obviously feels strongly about annuities.

On the other hand, you hear people from the academic community such as Robert Shiller, who is an American Nobel Prize winning economist, a professor of economics at Yale University, and has been ranked as one of the 100 most influential economists in the world, in his book *Irrational Exuberance* (the 2nd edition on page 222) say, "Authorities who are responsible for pension plans, including agencies like the Pension Benefit Guarantee

Corporation in the United States or the Pension Protection Fund in the United Kingdom, should come out strongly against over-reliance on the stock market. They should instead recommend greater diversification and suggest that a substantial fraction of balances be put into safe investments such as inflation-indexed government bonds, and they should promote inflation-indexed retirement annuities and urge retirees to take the retirement income in this form."

Then there is Harold Evensky, who has been called the "Father of Financial Planning" and manages $1.5 billion dollars of investment assets. He was a long time opponent of annuities, but has recently changed his mind when it comes to them. He says, "Immediate annuities will be the most important investment of the next decade." That's incredible. For somebody that was anti-annuity and formerly shunned them, to make a 180 degree change on using annuities in a portfolio for retirement income, has garnered a lot of people's attention.[2]

Roger Ibbotson, who is a professor emeritus at Yale school of management and a 10 time recipient of Graham & Dodd Awards for financial research excellence, and his team at Zebra Capital Management recently published a white paper titled *Fixed Indexed Annuities: Consider the Alternative.*

Ibbotson's latest research suggests that an FIA (uncapped and subject to a spread) helps control equity market risk and mitigate longevity risk.

---

2   https://www.thinkadvisor.com/2015/03/24/
    evensky-in-reversal-sees-annuities-as-vital-for-
    re/?slreturn=20180305131417

"Conventional wisdom has most investors de-risking their portfolios by allocating more heavily to bonds as they approach retirement," continued Ibbotson. "However, investors should consider other alternatives such as FIAs. In this low interest rate environment, complacency can be a danger to our clients' futures." [3]

With billions of dollars flowing into annuity contracts every year and the academic community speaking positively about their use, is it possible that there could be a place for annuities in retirement income planning?

With all financial vehicles there are pros and cons. Annuities are contract driven so you need to understand the terms of each contract you are considering, and they are not right for everyone.

Making statements like "I hate annuities" or "I love annuities" is not what is needed. What we need are financial advisers who are well-versed in all of the financial tools available so they can help the people they serve navigate these different financial vehicles as they prepare to make a transition from accumulating assets to converting their assets into an income stream that needs to last a lifetime.

Lets explore annuities in greater depth.

---

3   https://www.prnewswire.com/news-releases/renowned-economist-roger-ibbotson-unveils-new-research-indicating-fixed-indexed-annuities-may-outperform-bonds-over-the-next-decade-300609670.html

WHAT ARE ANNUITIES?

An annuity is a contract between you and an insurance company. Generally speaking, annuities are either immediate or deferred. An immediate annuity generates income right away. A deferred annuity may pay income in the future and deferred annuities are also tax deferred. Sometimes people buy a deferred annuity and never start the income. They just allow the account to grow in a tax-deferred status. Tax deferred means you don't pay taxes on the interest you earn until you withdraw money from the contract. When you do withdraw money, it is subject to ordinary income taxes, and if you are under age 59-1/2, then you may also be subject to an additional 10 percent federal penalty.

What are the different types of annuities?

Immediate annuities are often called single premium immediate annuities (SPIA). SPIAs are designed to generate income on a guaranteed basis. Essentially you give the insurance company a lump sum of money, and they guarantee you an income stream. The income can be guaranteed for a lifetime or for a certain number of years (known as period certain) like 5 years because you are laddering your income stream in retirement.

Deferred annuities generally do not produce any immediate income, although they could. Deferred annuities are designed to grow until income is needed. These deferred annuities generally come in three flavors:

- You can purchase a deferred fixed annuity that pays a fixed rate of interest.

- You can purchase a variable annuity, where your money is invested in the market using "sub-accounts", which ultimately invest in underlying mutual funds. Your value will fluctuate with the market, and you can lose money.

- Or, you can purchase a fixed index annuity (FIA), which provides a minimum guaranteed interest rate (usually 0-1 percent), and allows you to earn interest tied to the performance of an external market index without having to invest in the market itself. FIAs are designed to help protect your principal from market loss, but allow you to earn interest based on positive changes in the market index.

Do annuities preserve principal?

The answer is both yes and no. There are a lot of different types of annuities, so it really depends on the contract you are purchasing. An annuity is a contract with an insurance company and is only as good as the financial strength of the company offering the contract.

Fixed annuities and single premium immediate annuities may also be covered by a state guarantee association if the annuities are not issued by fraternal organizations. Each state has its own guarantee association, and you can learn more at **www.nolhga.com**.

Fluctuations in the value of variable annuities, where a consumer has agreed to bear market risk, are generally not covered by any guarantee association. However certain guarantees offered by variable annuities might be covered and may come at additional costs. These annuities are designed to fluctuate based on market conditions.

Who should buy an annuity?

From my experience, people who purchase annuities tend to be more conservative and do not want to gamble or risk all of their income needs in retirement to the whims of the stock market. If you think about it, when you buy an annuity contract you are basically buying insurance on your income. We tend to insure the things that are important to us. We insure our homes so if our home burns down we would not need to deplete our life savings to rebuild our house. We insure our lives so that if we die our loved ones will have the resources they need to be able to manage the transition. We insure our health so that if we get very sick our life savings is protected from a catastrophic loss, and we pool resources with other insureds to make sure we have the care we need and do not lose every penny we have saved due to a health crisis.

When you buy an annuity you are insuring your income needs. Generally the risks to your income are inflation, longevity, and stock market volatility. An insurance company can pool life expectancy risks to help make sure you never have to worry about running out of income in retirement. Visit **http://www.gao.gov/new.items/d11400.pdf** to view a report that was released in 2011 by the Government Accountability Office (GAO) that explores retirement income and the use of annuities.

How can you find the right annuity?

One of the reasons annuities are hard to shop for is because a lot of contracts, features, options, and riders are available and annuity contracts can be complicated and hard to understand. To make matters even more confusing, they are regulated by the state you live in and not the federal government. So different annuities will be available to you depending on where you live.

The most important thing you can do is find an independent licensed insurance agent who has the ability to shop multiple companies to help you find the right annuity for your situation. Try to get quotes from more than one person. Make sure you find an agent who explains both the advantages and disadvantages of the contract you are considering.

Many times agents have a reputation for telling you all about the benefits of annuities and leaving out the specifics about the downsides of the contracts. A perfect investment or insurance contract does not exist. Every financial vehicle has advantages and disadvantages, and it's important to weigh all of the benefits as well as the risks and fees to make sure the contract is not only appropriate but also the right option available for you.

What is the purpose of the money?

Before you buy an annuity, you should be able to answer this question, "What is the purpose of your money?"

Oftentimes when I am meeting with folks and ask them what is the purpose of the money they have saved for retirement, they will tell me first and foremost the purpose is to provide for their retirement. This is usually in the form of income. If you are looking for income, principal preservation and guarantees then a fixed or fixed indexed annuity might be a good fit.

Why should you purchase an annuity?

I've found one of the best use for annuities is to help solve for the retirement income gap. The retirement income gap is basically the difference between your budget and guaranteed income sources such as Social Security or a pension. For example, if you have Social Security of $2,000 per month and a budget that requires $5,000 per month of retirement income, then the gap is $3,000 per month.

An annuity or sometimes laddering annuities can be a very smart and cost-effective way of making sure you will have the income you need on an inflation-adjusted basis without having to worry about interest rates rising or the stock market crashing.

What happens to an annuity when you die?

I know you won't like this answer, but it depends. Remember annuities are contract driven, so you need to ask the agent you are working with about death benefits. The reason people ask this question is because in the old days, when you purchased a guaranteed income stream from an insurance company, if you died your heirs would not receive any benefit. So, if you bought a lifetime single premium immediate annuity today and died in one week there may not be a benefit for your heirs.

Insurance company annuity contracts have changed and evolved a lot since the old days of annuities. Today, many annuity contracts allow for income and also have death benefit provisions. It's important that you know how your annuity works. It is still possible to buy the old type of annuity that would not provide any benefit to your heirs, but in my experience I've found that most people do not want those contracts.

What about annuity fees?

This is a great question and one that most agents do not like to talk about. All annuities have some kind of fee structure. In my experience, variable annuities seem to have a reputation for the highest fee structure. When reviewing variable annuity contracts, I've found some that have had ongoing annual fees as high as 3.5 percent per year.

Single premium immediate annuities and fixed deferred annuities generally don't have an ongoing management fee.

While the fees specifically identified in fixed annuities are few, it doesn't mean they don't exist as insurance companies are not required to disclose all of their costs on fixed products. The product's pricing is built into its caps, spreads, interest rates, payout rates, commissions, and more - on top of actual rider and surrender charge fees.

Single premium immediate annuities also have what I call a "liquidity cost". Once you start the income, you lose access to the principal for a lump sum distribution. This may not be a direct fee, but it certainly could be considered an opportunity cost because you lose out on the opportunity to have access to the contract for a lump sum distribution. Many fixed deferred annuities usually carry a surrender charge. The nice thing about a surrender charge is that you only pay that fee if you take more than a certain percentage per year.

How do taxes work with annuities?

Annuities are generally tax deferred. You do not get a tax benefit for contributing to an annuity like you would with a traditional IRA, but the money in a deferred annuity will grow tax deferred just like it would in an IRA.

How you take money out of an annuity will determine the tax at the time of withdrawal. If you just take a withdrawal from an annuity it is taxed using LIFO tax treatment — last in, first out. So your interest comes out first, and your interest is taxed at ordinary income tax rates. Your ultimate tax would be determined by the effective tax rate for that year.

If you annuitize a contract and have the annuity pay out over a lifetime or a period certain, then the IRS allows you to use the exclusion ratio. The exclusion ratio is basically a formula the IRS will use to determine which portion of the income you receive is considered interest earned versus a return of principal. This is the most tax efficient way to get money back out of an annuity over a number of years, and it can also be a good way to generate cash flow on a tax-favorable basis.

Should you purchase an annuity inside of an IRA?

From a tax planning standpoint there is no additional tax benefit by holding an annuity inside an IRA. An IRA is tax deferred, and so is an annuity. There is no such thing as double tax deferral.

However, many people will use an annuity to fund an IRA because they are interested in the guarantees being offered by the insurance company. Some people would argue that it makes sense to hold your at-risk investments in non-qualified accounts rather than an IRA or 401k because in years where you lose money, you can deduct the losses from non-qualified accounts on your tax return. If your IRA were invested in an at-risk position and you lose money, then you generally cannot deduct the losses on your tax return. There are many instances where it may make sense to hold an annuity in an IRA, but doing so for tax reasons is not one of them.

How can I find competitive annuity rates?

Because annuities are regulated by each state, no single website exists that can provide all of the rates available. Our advice is to contact more than one independent agent and ask them to shop rates for you. The annuity marketplace is very competitive and insurance companies want to try and win your business, so it will usually pay off to put in some extra research.

FIXED INDEXED ANNUITIES

A Fixed Indexed Annuity (FIAs) is a contract with an insurance company that offers some unique features.

- are considered a safe place for money.

- are guaranteed against loss of principal.

- guarantee a minimum rate of return/worse case.

- have the ability to earn a return greater than the minimum guarantee based on the upward movement of a stock market index such as the S&P 500 or the DJIA.

- give you greater control of your tax liability with the available tax deferral option.

- ends at death so your beneficiaries receive the account value without having to hold the position until maturity.

- when structured properly, will bypass probate and go directly to your named beneficiaries.

- have liquidity features allowing you to access your account value at any time. Ninety percent of your money is usually available, while 10 percent could be eaten up by surrender charges if you were to pull all of your money out in the first year. On the flip side, you can access 10 percent of the account value every year without any type of surrender charge or penalty.

FIAs offer many attractive features for the average retiree. Now, downsides do exist for these tools, so you should request the product brochures and know the financial strength of the company issuing them before you make a decision.

Because Fixed Indexed Annuities will credit interest based on the stock market's movement, they can be a good way to perserve principal and to hedge against inflation risk. In a 2009 interview with *Annuity Digest*, David Babbel, a Wharton professor who had recently conducted a study about FIAs, stated:

> The in-depth studies we conducted took over two years to complete and involved six Ph.D. financial economists and a pair of very well known senior actuaries. Our studies show that the products of at least some of the companies

in this field are viable—indeed, rather attractive products. Our findings regarding actual products show that since their inception in 1995, they have performed quite well—in fact, some have performed better than many alternative investment classes (corporate and government bonds, equity funds, money markets) in any combination.[4]

As I researched FIAs, I came across an October 2009 report titled "Real World Index Annuity Returns" by the Wharton Financial Institutions Center. The paper was written by David Babbel, as well as Jack Marrion and Geoffrey VanderPal. Now these guys have some pretty impressive credentials. Jack Marrion is an MBA doctoral candidate in the area of cognitive bias in decision-making and is president of Advantage Compendium. Geoffrey VanderPal, DBA, MBA, CLU, CFS, RFC, CTP, CAMS, is the Chief Investment officer of Skyline Capital Management. David Babbel is a professor of insurance and finance at the Wharton School of Business, University of Pennsylvania, a Senior-Adviser to Charles River Associates, and a fellow of the Wharton Financial Institutions Center. The entire report is very interesting and available online for download at the Wharton Financial Institutions Center's website.[5]

Page 6 of this report, paragraph 4, states, "From 1997 through 2007 the five-year annualized returns for FIAs averaged 5.79 percent. This compares to 5.39 percent for taxable bond funds and 4.73 percent for fixed annuities."

---

4 http://www.annuitydigest.com/blog/tom/interview-wharton-professor-david-babbel-part-one. Accessed February 12, 2011.

5 http://fic.wharton.upenn.edu/fic/Policy percent20page/RealWorldReturns.pdf. Accessed February 12, 2011.

These numbers were based on actual customer statements and from a limited number of contracts. You should read this report in its entirety, but what is important is that it provides information on how these contracts actually performed—not how they hypothetically would have performed.

Here are some important questions to ask yourself: Has your adviser ever mentioned this type of product to you? And do you currently own bonds or bond mutual funds in your investment portfolio?

The reality is that these tools, when utilized properly, can provide an alternative to a bond portfolio. My experience tells me that many advisers don't make these tools available to their clients. But it's not the advisers' faults. Many of the folks in my community work for large Wall Street-owned corporations that determine what is and what is not available for their clients.

For this reason, I believe you should choose to work with an independent advisory firm that acts in a fiduciary capacity by conducting business or handling property for the benefit of another person. The advisers are responsible for proving, if asked, that they acted in their clients' best interests, not their own. Many independent advisory firms are registered investment advisers (RIAs). RIAs are registered with either the State Department of Finance or the U.S. Securities and Exchange Commission, which manages the investments of others. This registration doesn't mean the adviser is recommended by the State or SEC, but it means he or she is regulated by the State or SEC. In general, an RIA with more than $100 million under management must register with the SEC. RIAs managing less than $100 million are registered at the state level.

By working with an independent advisory firm that is an RIA, you know you are working with a firm that will always work in your best interest, and because of its independence, it will have access to all of the products available and not just those the corporation allows.

UNDERSTANDING THE SPIA

A SPIA is a Single Premium Immediate Annuity contract. These contracts have been designed by insurance companies to provide a guaranteed income stream. Chances are, if you have a pension from your employer, you already have a SPIA. The company most likely purchased an insurance contract that guarantees your monthly income payments for the remainder of your life. In my opinion, SPIAs are one of the most underutilized annuity contracts. The academic world has long sung their praises and a report in 2011 by the U.S. Government Accountability Office (U.S. GAO) suggests retirees consider delaying Social Security and opting for an annuity rather than a lump sum from an employer plan.

A SPIA helps insure against an individual outliving his or her retirement income. SPIAs can be structured to provide a guaranteed income for a surviving spouse as well. SPIAs are offered by insurance companies; in a recent interview with a very large insurance company, the insurance company representative said people used to go to insurance companies to help protect against the risk of dying too soon. Now insurance companies are helping to protect against the risk of living too long.

The S&P 500 tumbled 46 percent during the freom the end of 2007 to the end of March 2009. Retirement is all about cash flow, not net worth. If you have a million dollars invested in the S&P 500 mutual funds, and you are pulling money from it for income, and your account drops 46 percent in one year, you will have some sleepless nights. A SPIA, if set up properly, could guarantee a percent of your income without having to rely on the stock market. Then when the volatile stock market drops, it won't be such a shock to your system.

The income you receive from a non-qualified SPIA account is also split by an exclusion ratio. A portion of the money is considered a return of premium and a portion of it is considered taxable interest income. SPIAs are very tax-efficient at creating income.

If you are thinking of buying bonds for income, be sure you can hold the bonds until maturity. Be careful with bond funds in a rising interest rate environment like we are in currently; that is the time to consider using a SPIA instead because it is guarantees income and can be more tax efficient than other options.

WHAT IS YOUR FIRST MEMORY OF MONEY?

I was recently asked the question, "What is your first memory of money?" As I started to think back to my childhood, I made it to about age 5 when I remember swimming in a lake with my mom and dad. My mom was sitting on the bank of the lake with my baby brother; I was splashing around in the shallow water with my dad. My dad would dive under the water and come back up with a silver dollar. I remember him pretending he had found a buried treasure chest full of them. He would hand the silver dollar to me, and I would run up and show my mom and shout, "Look we found another one." Then I would turn and run back into the water where my dad would dive under the water and come up with another silver dollar. Little did I know at the time that my dad had a pocket full of silver dollars and there was no buried treasure. But for me, at age 5, it was a real adventure. I cherish that memory, but I'm not sure I would have recalled it if I had never been asked the question.

So lately, I've been asking just about everybody I meet that question. Many of the people we serve had parents who lost all of their savings during the Great Depression. And it's interesting to hear how that loss impacted them. In some cases they remember their parents being very tight with money and saving everything they could get their hands on. In other instances they remember their parents adopted a "live for the day" mentality. They didn't save much because they figured they could lose it all at any time, so what was the sense in saving. I've heard stories about how people remember their parents handing them a nickel to put in the offering plate every Sunday morning at church. One gentleman told me a story about walking down to the corner store when he was probably about six years old and buying two eggs with the six cents his mom had given him. Then, on the way home, the eggs broke, and he got into a lot of trouble.

Money has in many instances played an important role in shaping our clients' lives. One gentleman told me that over his working years he had "traded his life's energy to accumulate wealth," and how important it was to him not squander his life's energy "in the pursuit of meaningless things." I really thought that was powerful, and it has stayed with me.

One of the things I love about the work I do is that I am able to ask our clients questions that help me understand and learn more about who they are and what is important them. These types of questions help me better understand the sacrifices that were made, the opportunities that were pursued, and ultimately who they had to become in order to achieve their financial success.

What an honor it is to be in the position to be able to ask these questions. I oftentimes say I am blessed to have the good fortune to learn important life lessons from some of the greatest people in all of Kitsap County and in some cases in the United States.

Chapter 5

TIPS FOR MAXIMIZING YOUR SOCIAL SECURITY BENEFIT

When Social Security started, the average life expectancy was 66. You couldn't start receiving your benefits until age 65. So what started out as old-age insurance and wasn't expected to be paid to very many people has blossomed into a very important retirement benefit. For the baby boomer generation, it is more important than ever because the boomers don't generally have pensions. Now the boomers have to rely on Social Security and their savings for a lifetime of income.

Based on the 2018 statements you receive every year from the Social Security Administration, by 2034, just before I am eligible for my Social Security benefits, Social Security will only be able to pay out 77 cents on the dollar unless changes are made to the system. So by then, if you had been receiving $1,000 per month in benefits, it is possible Social Security would reduce your benefit to $770 per month.

If you have the forty credits of work required to qualify for your benefits, you can begin drawing your benefit at age 62. However, by beginning at age 62, your Social Security benefit will be about 25 percent less (for those born between 1943-1954) than it will be if you wait until your full retirement age, which for most baby boomers will be age 66.

Every year you wait to start your benefits beyond age 66 increases your benefits by 8 percent until you reach age 70. Remember, if you begin drawing benefits at age 62, you are limited on how much income you can earn in one year before Social Security reduces your benefits. For example, in 2018 you could earn $17,040. After the $17,040 threshold has been met, your benefits would be reduced by $1 for every $2 in other earnings. So if you plan to work beyond age 62, it might make sense to delay taking your benefits. Visit **www.ssa.gov** for updated threshold amounts.

Those born between 1943 and 1954 will be eligible for their full retirement benefits at age 66. At this time, you can earn as much money as you like without worrying about your benefits being reduced. Nor are you required to take your benefits at age 66. In fact, every month you wait to take them, you will earn bonus credits at about 0.66 percent more each month. If you were to delay taking your benefits until age seventy, you could have as much as 132 percent of your full retirement benefit.

QUALITY VS QUANTITY

An affluent client who was quickly approaching age 62 recently asked my opinion about when he and his wife should begin taking Social Security. My initial response was based on much of the analyses I've done about how one can actuarially maximize Social Security benefits over two people's lives. By understanding the rules and structuring Social Security in such a way that you are taking full advantage of all of the nuances within the system, a married couple can greatly increase the amount of benefits received over two people's lifetime. Sometimes we geeky number guys are more concerned with the math than the reality of how the choice impacts lifestyle.

This client pointed out that he and his wife have plenty of income from other sources, and Social Security will just be an added bonus. He also pointed out that if he used the strategies we teach to maximize his Social Security benefits it may mean he would receive more money from the Social Security administration over both of their lifetimes, but most of that additional money would come much later in life. He said, "If I start taking my Social Security at age 62, I have several very good years to really enjoy the extra infusion of cash. This extra money would afford us more travel and spending more time with our kids and grandkids. That additional income while we are young is much more important to us from a lifestyle standpoint than having an increased income when we are in our 80s."

I was reminded that a one-size-fits-all approach to retirement planning doesn't work. We really need to create a plan based upon your financial reality. Just because we can help you receive an additional $50,000 of Social Security income over the lifetime of you and your wife, doesn't mean that it is what is best for your situation. The additional funds may not matter if you are receiving it at a time when you won't be able to enjoy it as much. Ultimately the question this couple was faced with was, "Do we begin taking Social Security early and enjoy a higher quality of life while we can, or do we wait to take benefits later so that we receive a higher quantity of money over our lifetime?"

Now the reality is that this couple has the flexibility to ask these types of questions and make these choices because they have done an excellent job preparing for retirement. Because they are affluent, high net worth couples, who have really good retirement income, have more options available to them.

I've also met with people where how and when they begin taking Social Security benefits is a determining factor for whether or not they are going to run out of money in retirement. So for many of the people we serve, the additional Social Security income later in life is really critical to the longevity of their resources.

Social Security benefits are tax-advantaged income, inflation adjusted, and have benefits for a surviving spouse. In many cases, a healthy couple retiring today will receive more than half a million dollars in lifetime benefits from the Social Security administration. It is good to know the strategies for how to maximize these benefits, but just because you can doesn't mean you should.

WHAT HAPPENS TO MY SOCIAL SECURITY WHEN I DIE?

If Mr. Smith is receiving $1,000 per month in Social Security income, and Mrs. Smith is receiving her spousal benefit of $500 dollars per month, then their total monthly benefit is $1,500 per month. If Mr. Smith dies, Mrs. Smith will stop receiving her benefit of $500 per month, and she will receive a step up to her husband's higher benefit (Survivor Benefit), making her total monthly income $1,000 per month. Because Mrs. Smith has a higher probability of living longer than Mr. Smith, they need to do some strategic planning to maximize the spousal benefit. If Mr. Smith delays taking his benefit until age 70, they would maximize the amount of money available in retirement for Mrs. Smith.

Because boomers are likely going to rely more heavily on their Social Security benefits than past generations, they need to look at all of the different ways they can maximize these benefits and find a good adviser who can help them create a plan for taking those Social Security benefits.

SOLVING FOR THE RETIREMENT INCOME GAP

The retirement income gap is simply the difference between your budget and your guaranteed income sources. For example, if you have a budget that requires $5,000 per month of income in today's dollars, and you have guaranteed income from Social Security and pensions of $3,000 per month then your gap is $2,000 per month.

One of the ways you can create the greatest amount of confidence in your retirement income plan is to solve for the gap using strategies that have the least amount of volatility. Each solution to solving for this gap has varying degrees of risk. If you are ultra conservative, then you might consider laddering certificates of deposit and living off the interest income to cover the gap. Or maybe you ladder annuity contracts and create guaranteed income using annuities.

If you are willing to assume more risk, then perhaps you would prefer to buy a diversified portfolio of individual corporate and treasury bonds and live off the income while planning to hold the bonds to maturity. Or, maybe if you are comfortable with even more risk, then you consider buying a diversified dividend-paying stock portfolio and only live off the income that is generated and never touch the principal.

Many ways exist to build a portfolio to solve for the gap, but the important thing is that you have a plan in place, you understand the risks associated with your plan, and you stick with the plan in good times and bad.

Getting caught up in the euphoria of the markets is easy. In good times, we get greedy and want more. In bad times, we want more safety and just don't want to lose our principal. If you don't stick with the plan, then you will always be shifting from one great idea to the next and will end up with very little confidence that your plan will work.

Most of the people we serve are conservative. They want to have a high degree of confidence that the numbers are going to work, regardless of market conditions, and so we tend to design plans starting with the most conservative options first and then, depending on each client's appetite for risk, we can assume more risk.

Retirement is all about cash flow, not your net worth. Your income is what will allow you to enjoy the lifestyle you have worked hard for. Designing a plan with the highest probability of success and the least amount of volatility helps most people feel better about their retirement income plan.

ONE WAY TO REDUCE TAXES ON SOCIAL SECURITY INCOME

Before we show you one way to reduce taxes on social security income, we need to determine if your social security income is taxable.

The easiest way to determine if your social security income will be taxable is to add one half of the social security income you received with all of your other taxable income sources including tax exempt interest. This is called your provisional income.

1/2 Social Security Income + all of your other taxable income including tax exempt interest (do not include Roth distributions) = provisional income

A little known, but powerful fact, is that qualified distributions from a Roth IRA are tax free and are not included in the income calculation for determining if your social security income is taxable. This could be a one more reason to consider converting a traditional IRA to a Roth IRA.

If you file an individual tax return in 2018 and your provisional income is between:

- $25,000 – $34,000 you may have to pay income taxes on up to 50 percent of your benefits.

- $34,000 or more and you may have to pay income taxes on up to 85 percent of your benefits.

If you file a joint tax return in 2018 and your provisional income is between:

- $32,000 – $44,000 You may have to pay income taxes on up to 50 percent of your benefits.

- $44,000 or more and you may have to pay income taxes on up to 85 percent of your benefits.

If your social security income is taxable, then here is a strategy for reducing those taxes:

One of the simplest ways to reduce taxation of social security is to reduce the amount of income you are receiving via a 1099, but that you are reinvesting instead of actually spending.

For example, if you are receiving 1099 interest income from your bank certificate of deposit and spending the income, then this little trick will not work.

However, if you have 1099 interest income from a bank certificate of deposit and you are not spending the income, but rather just rolling the interest back into the CD, then you could potentially reduce your tax liability by utilizing either **tax-deferred annuities or tax-deferred savings bonds.**

In our example below, we assume that Mr. & Mrs. Tax have $20,000 of 1099 interest income from their certificates of deposit. Mr. & Mrs. Tax explained that they do not use any of the interest income that is being generated from their portfolio of CD's to satisfy their lifestyle needs. All of the interest income is being reinvested.

If they use a fixed tax-deferred annuity contract, then they would still earn interest on their money, possibly even more interest, and the interest income would not be included in their taxable income until they took a withdrawal from the account and received income, so no 1099 until they pulled funds from that account.

By choosing when you draw income from a fixed-deferred annuity contract, you can have more control over when you pay taxes, which you can use to influence how much of your social security income is taxable in a given year.

You can see from our tax spreadsheet below (highlighted in blue) that this simple trick could reduce the amount of social security that is being taxed from **49 percent to only 11 percent** of benefits.

But even more important in this scenario is the clients annual tax bill is reduced from $4,755 per year to only $180 dollars per year. Reducing their effective tax rate from 7.9 percent to only 0.7 percent.

This shows you how income that is being reported, but not necessarily spent, can have a negative impact not just on the amount of your social security income that is taxed, but also the bottom line in terms of the amount of federal income tax you pay every year.

When creating a retirement cash flow plan be sure to take into consideration the impact taxes will have on your income.

Cash Flow and Taxes for:	Mr & Mrs Tax				
Prepared by: Jason Parker			Date: Oct. 5, 2015		
Tax Filing	joint 2014		joint 2014		
Tax Module					

Income	Current		Tax Deferred Interest		
	Cash Flow	Tax Return	Cash Flow	Tax Return	
Interest (8a)	20,000	20,000	0	0	
IRA Distributions (15)	20,000	20,000	20,000	20,000	
His Social Security (20)	24,000	18,000	24,000		
Her Social Security (20)	18,000		18,000		
Total Social Security	42,000	20,450 49%	42,000	4,500 11%	
Income Sub Total	$ 82,000.00	60,450	$ 62,000.00	24,500	
Expenses					
Expenses Sub Total	$ -		$ -		
Income Taxes					
Personal Exemption	0	7,900	0	7,900	
Standard Deduction		14,800		14,800	
Largest Deduction - Schedule A or Standard		14,800		14,800	
TAXABLE INCOME	15% Tax Bracket	37,750 Eff Rate	10% Tax Bracket	1,800 Eff Rate	
Total Social Security		4,755 7.9%		180 0.7%	
Discretionary Income	$ 77,245.00		$ 61,820.00		

Above example shown for illustrative purposes only and does not reflect an actual client or investment portfolio.

I've learned that most people do not mind paying their fair share of taxes, but most people do not want to pay more than their fair share.

Social Security Taxation

Social Security income has not always been taxable. Take a look at how political parties have impacted the taxation of your social security retirement income.

Which political party is responsible for the taxation of social security?[1]

In 1983 congress voted on amendments that were proposed by the Greenspan commission to allow up to 50 percent of social security

---

1   http://www.ssa.gov/history/InternetMyths2.html
    http://www.irs.gov/uac/Newsroom/Are-Your-Social-Security-Benefits-Taxable
    http://www.irs.gov/uac/Are-Your-Social-Security-Benefits-Taxable%3F
    http://www.ssa.gov/planners/taxes.html

to be included in taxable income if certain income thresholds were met. Ronald Reagan signed this legislation in 1983 and social security retirement income taxation began in 1984. The Senate majority in 1983 was the Republican Party and the House Majority was the Democratic Party.

In 1993 legislation was enacted and signed into law under President Clinton that increased the amount of social security that could be taxed from 50 percent up to 85 percent. The Senate Majority Party was the Democratic Party. The House Majority Party was the Democratic Party.

SOCIAL SECURITY CLAIMING STRATEGIES HAVE CHANGED

On November 2, 2015 President Obama signed a budget deal that dramatically changed Social Security claiming rules. For many Americans Social Security is the foundation of a good retirement income plan. These changes to Social Security underscore the importance of having a good retirement cash flow plan that is flexible and can withstand public policy risks.

Under the old law there were two primary claiming strategies that were commonly known as "File and Suspend" and the "Restricted Application." We had been able to help many retirees plan to increase their lifetime social security income by understanding how to structure claiming strategies that maximized benefits over two peoples lifetime. In many instances this planning had the potential to significantly increase projected lifetime income from Social Security.

The new budget deal has phased out the "File and Suspend" and limited the "Restricted Application" strategies to those born before 1954. Below are a few highlights that may be important to your retirement income plan.

Restricted Application for Spousal Benefits:

The old law would allow you to file a restricted application in order to restrict taking your own benefit and instead receive just a spousal benefit based on your spouses earnings record. By filing a restricted application at your full retirement age, you would allow your own social security benefit to earn the 8 percent delayed retirement credits. At age 70 you would switch from your spousal benefit to your own benefit.

The new law that has passed will begin phasing the restricted application strategy out. For people who were born before January 1, 1954 the option to file for only spousal benefits will continue. However for those who were born January 2, 1954 and later, an application for spousal benefits will automatically trigger entitlement to all other benefits. So you will no longer be able to file a restricted application and only receive your spousal benefits while delaying taking your own benefit if you were born after January 1, 1954.

File & Suspend:

Under the old law you could voluntarily suspend your benefits. If you were full retirement age you could elect to file/activate your benefit and then put your benefit into suspense. This would allow your own benefit to continue to earn 8 percent per year delayed retirement credits and by activating your benefits it also gave your spouse, who was full retirement age, more claiming options. Because you had filed for benefits, your spouse became eligible for spousal benefits based on your earnings record. Your spouse then had the choice of restricting their application to file only for spousal benefits or file for their own benefit.

The new law causes all benefits to stop being paid under a voluntary suspension. So if you suspend taking your own benefit, then your spouse will no longer be able to collect a spousal benefit during the time your benefit is suspended.

The old law said that if you filed for your benefits at age 66 and put them into suspense, you could file for a lump sum of deferred benefits at a future time. The new law also eliminates the ability to request a lump sum of benefits.

The good new is that if you filed for these benefits and put them into suspense before April 30, 2016, then you are grandfathered in under the old law until you reach age 70 or un-suspend your benefits.

Widow Benefits:

The good news is that the new law did not impact widow benefits. Widows will continue to have the flexibility to restrict their application.

For some of the people we have served, a good Social Security claiming strategy made the difference between being able to retire with confidence rather than worry about potentially running out of money in retirement.

I think it is important to remember that our elected leaders literally changed the rules overnight.

SOCIAL SECURITY CALCULATORS

Visit the below link to watch a short video where we explain why married couples who use a social security calculator could receive as much as an additional $50,000 of lifetime benefits.

http://soundretirementplanning.com/benefits-social-security-calculator/

Social Security income is tax-advantaged income, inflation-adjusted income and has a benefit for a surviving spouse.

In some instances I've seen where a poor choice when electing benefits could be the difference between having enough money for retirement or running out of money early.

I am reminded that a one-size-fits-all approach to retirement planning doesn't work. We really need to create a plan based upon your financial reality. Just because we could help you receive an additional $50,000 in Social Security income over the lifetime of you and your spouse, doesn't mean that it is best for your situation. The additional funds may not matter if you are receiving it at a time when you won't be able to enjoy it much. Ultimately the question becomes, "Do we begin taking Social Security early and enjoy a higher quality of life while we can, or do we wait to take benefits later so that we receive a higher quantity of money over our lifetime?"

DO YOU HAVE A SOCIAL SECURITY BACK-UP PLAN? PLANNING FOR REDUCED BENEFITS

Should you have a Social Security back-up plan for income?

I like to have a contingency plan in place for the "What if's" in life; for those times when life throws us a curve ball.

For example, at my home we keep two weeks of food, fuel and water on hand in case of an emergency.

At work, I continuously back-up my computer because if my hard drive fails, then I want to make sure we have a back-up plan to ensure our business can continue to operate uninterrupted.

I also buy insurance to protect my family from a financial emergency. Should I die, become disabled, have a major health insurance expense, get into a car accident, have our house burn down, or need long-term care, then I have insurance aka a back-up plan in place to make sure my family is protected.

Should you have a backup plan in place in the event that the social security trustees report is accurate with their warning that they will only be able to pay 77 percent of scheduled benefits by the year 2034?

Let's take a quick look at how these projected reduced benefits might impact a man retiring in the year 2015.

For this example let's assume Mr. Jones is 66 years old and he just started his social security retirement income of $2000 per month in the year 2015.

If we assume that his social security benefit will increase by the historical cost of living allowance of 2.5 percent per year, then we would project by the year 2033 his monthly scheduled benefit would have increased to $3,119 per month. He would now be 84 years old.

If we then apply the social security trustee's projected reduction in benefits and assume that social security will only be able to pay 77 percent of his scheduled benefits, then this is how that reduction would impact his retirement cash flow.

- $717 dollars of lost income per month. His monthly income would drop from $3,119 to $2,402.

- $8,609 dollars less retirement income per year.

- If he lives to age 95 and the reduction holds steady he will have received $118,770 less in income.

For many Americans Social Security will replace 40 percent of their annual pre-retirement earnings.

If your retirement plan is dependent on collecting social security income, then it may be prudent to consider a back-up plan to ensure you will have enough inflation-adjusted income to last for your lifetime should the social security trustee's analyses become a reality.

Chapter 6

DIVERSIFYING IN A RETIREMENT INCOME STRATEGY

I've explained the different money worlds, and how to create a diversified portfolio. Let's use the same concepts but build a portfolio for retirement **income**.

By diversifying assets by time as well as risk, you create a structure that can help you stay invested in good times and bad. At my firm, I want to know how my clients feel about risk. If I have an ultra-conservative client who is not comfortable at all with stock market risk, then I recommend a very conservative strategy. If a client has a higher propensity for risk, then I recommend a strategy that provides for the opportunity to earn the greatest return.

THE MORE AGGRESSIVE APPROACH TO RETIREMENT INCOME

Some people we work with have an aversion to certain tools or products. We have people who come into our office who are absolutely opposed to using annuities. Either they have had a bad experience with them, or they have read enough of the negative media that they do not want to consider them in their plan. We're fine with that. You need to let your adviser know about these concerns or aversions before a plan is built. If a client tells me he or she doesn't like or understand annuities and would prefer not to use them, then we don't use them.

Maybe instead, you ladder CDs over a seven-year time span in the first segment. Then in the second segment, you would use a tactical money management conservative portfolio. In the third segment, you would use a strategic investment manager with a conservative growth asset allocation. The fourth and fifth segments, because you have the most time on your side, would use a strategic asset allocation moderate growth strategy and strategically rebalance.

The key is to have a plan and make sure you are working with an adviser who understands the difference between how you should invest your money when accumulating assets versus establishing a plan for the distribution and income phase of your retirement life. Find someone who is flexible and has the ability to do things the way you want them done.

My clients should view me as a coach. They tell me what it is they are trying to accomplish, and I show them a couple of different ways they can achieve their goals. If I am the coach, ultimately, they are the general managers and have to decide which way is best for them.

A TRADITIONAL 60/40 APPROACH TO RETIREMENT INCOME

I met some folks recently who wanted to use more of a traditional 60/40 approach to their retirement income planning, and they were comfortable accepting the risks associated with it. They explained they had an aversion to annuity contracts and when constructing their retirement income plan they did not want to use any.

My job as an adviser is to listen to people and help them do things the way they want them done. I'm fond of the old saying, "God gave us two ears and one mouth so that we would spend more time listening and less time talking." I also have a responsibility to help highlight the risks, fees, taxes, and other consequences of the choices people are considering. You want to make sure you find an adviser who has the flexibility to help you accomplish your goals the way you want to accomplish them. While I feel strongly about the systems we have created to help diversify both their time horizon as well as the products they use, I recognize some people have a different vision for accomplishing their goals, and that is OK. This is your retirement, and you should do it your way.

After several meetings and a lengthy discussion, they liked the idea of allocating about sixty percent of their portfolio to actively managed individual bonds and about forty percent of their portfolio allocated to an actively managed portfolio of individual dividend-paying stocks.

We talked about the risks associated with both stocks and bonds. These folks said, "Jason we do not really care about market fluctuations or what the value of the portfolio is at any one time as long as it is consistently producing the income we need. That is all we really care about."

In the past I've discussed the disadvantages of buying bonds in a low interest rate environment. If you are going to buy bonds today, then I prefer owning individual bonds over bond mutual funds. In a rising interest rate environment, I'm concerned we could see a mad dash for the exit as people begin to lose money in bond funds due to rising interest rates. If a lot of people exit a bond mutual fund all at once, then it could cause a bond fund manager to liquidate positions to raise cash.

At least with an individual bond you have the ability to hold that bond until maturity. You have control over when it is sold. You may see the market value of the bond drop as a result of rising interest rates, but as long as you hold the bond to maturity and the company issuing the bond does not default, then you would have received all of the income over the term of the bond. Plus at maturity you would get back the value of the bond plus or minus your initial investment, depending on if you had purchased the bond at a premium, at a discount, or at par.

The nice thing about the dividend stock portfolio we constructed is the portfolio of individual dividend-paying stocks have a history of increasing their dividends. No guarantees exist that the companies will continue to pay their dividends or increase their dividends, but having the potential for dividend increases and buying companies that have a track record of raising their dividends can help provide for a hedge against inflation. Many companies have paid dividends for years. Once a company starts paying a dividend, they generally want to keep paying the dividend because, if they stop, it can have a negative impact on the company and the management. In some instances it can cause shareholders to exit their positions.

The key to this approach is that you need to accept the risks associated with it. The portfolio will fluctuate, and in some years those fluctuations can be great. But if you are like these folks, you don't really care what the value of the portfolio is from year to year, and income is your primary concern, then this can be a great way to create a diversified portfolio that is geared to help you meet your goals.

Chapter 7

THE IMPORTANCE OF FEES

Stop paying high commissions and fees for your mutual funds. Just stop it!

Okay, I've got that out of my system so let's move on. You need to understand the impact fees can have on your investment portfolio. I believe by diversifying your investments as suggested in the previous chapters, you are diversifying your investments for principal preservation and growth, but you are also moving your investments to very fee-efficient accounts. If you had all your investments in no-load mutual funds, and the average fee on those mutual funds was 1 percent per year on $100,000, your annual expense would be $1,000. If you currently own mutual funds, it can be hard to uncover all of the fees you are paying. Of course, your prospectus will list fees, but a quick way to help uncover all of the fees you are paying is to use a tool at **www.personalfund.com**.

EXCHANGE TRADED FUNDS (ETFS) VS. MUTUAL FUNDS

I am fan of low cost investing using asset allocation as the foundation for maximizing risk adjusted returns. Jack Bogle of Vanguard is one of my personal heroes in our industry and an advocate for the smaller investor. Vanguard built its firm around low cost Indexed Mutual Funds, and now Vanguard is one of the leaders in the Exchange Traded Funds (ETFs) arena. Both vehicles have advantages and disadvantages.

One common complaint about ETFs is the brokerage fees associated with buying and selling these investments. If you intend to do a lot of buying and selling within the portfolio of ETFs, then you should use a more fee-efficient tool to track an index, like the ETFs' close cousin the Index Mutual Fund, instead.

However, I have found ETFs have lower costs, are more liquid, and can be very tax efficient, which is very important for your non-qualified accounts. Either choice serves the same basic purpose. Both are excellent vehicles for helping you achieve your long-term growth goals.

ETFs and Indexed Mutual Funds, are both very efficient tools for creating global broad-based diversified portfolios among asset classes and sectors, and they should be considered as a part of your overall diversification strategy.

BRAIN SURGERY

Do you remember the first time you had to make a life or death decision? About 20 years ago I was working for the state of Alaska when my telephone rang. It was my wife. She did not usually call me at work, but this particular day was our one-year wedding anniversary, so I figured she was calling to wish me a happy anniversary. Instead she said, "Jason, I was at my mom's house when she fell over and hit her head on a table, and she's bleeding.

I called the ambulance and we're on our way to the hospital. Can you meet us there?"

When I arrived at the hospital, I learned my mother-in-law had a very bad headache. She was only in her mid 50s and had never been sick a day in her life, so this was very unusual. The doctors thought the headache was because of her fall. She also had a small cut under her eye where she had been bleeding. My wife and I sat in the waiting room for what seemed like an eternity, but in all reality was probably not very long.

We tried to call my father-in-law, but he was out of town on a business trip. We couldn't track him down. I remember walking back to where my mother-in-law was laying in the hospital bed, and I asked her how she was doing. She just reached up holding her head and said, "My head hurts so bad." The doctors initially thought she was having a migraine. A short while later the doctors walked into the waiting room and let my wife and I know that they had done a scan of my mother-in-law's brain. The doctor said it looked like she had bleeding in her brain. He said she was going to need brain surgery. He went on to explain that they didn't do brain surgery in Juneau, Alaska, so we would need to decide whether to have her flown to Anchorage or to Seattle for it.

He went on to say that Seattle would be a little longer flight. I remember staring into the doctor's eyes because this was the first time in my life where I felt I was making a life or death decision on behalf of another person. I looked at the doctor and I asked him, "Who has the best brain surgeon in the world?" With my father-in-law out of town, I knew if my wife and I had to make this decision we wanted the absolute best.

The doctor looked at me and told me the best brain surgeon in the world was in Seattle. Shortly thereafter my wife and my mother-in-law were on a high-speed jet flying from Juneau, Alaska to Seattle, Washington. And it turned out, Seattle did indeed have one of the best brain surgeons in the world. I'm very happy to report that 20 years after having brain surgery, my mother-in-law has made a full recovery and lives 5 minutes from us. It is wonderful to have Grandma nearby to love on our kids.

As this story relates to retirement planning, the important lesson I learned that day was in the power of the question I asked, "Who had the best brain surgeon in the world?" I didn't ask who had the best cardiologist. I didn't ask who had the best general practitioner. I didn't ask my coworkers, family, or friends to perform the surgery. I wanted the best brain surgeon in the world. I wanted somebody who did brain surgery day in and day out, 365 days a year.

One of the mistakes we see many people make when working on their retirement planning is they ask the advice of a family member, friend, coworker, or even a general practitioner financial advice giver. While all of these people may certainly mean well, chances are they don't know all the specifics to your circumstances to truly give you expert advice. Really all they are equipped to do is to tell you what worked for them and offer an opinion.

Retirement involves many different areas of expertise. You must consider how to maximize your Social Security, pensions, and other income sources as well as create tax-efficient income. A financial adviser should be trained in how to preserve a lifetime of hard work and wealth and make sure you don't run out of money during your lifetime. A skilled practitioner will be looking at your investments, insurance, estate plan, entitlements, pensions, inflation, and taxes to make sure every area of your financial life is coordinated and optimized, so you will confidently meet your goals.

The decisions you make as you transition into and through retirement will be some of the most important that you may ever make. Remember you may spend as many years retired as you did working. Twenty-five years of unemployment is a long time, and you won't be adding to your investments any more. What you have is what you have, and you need to make sure it is going to last as long as you do.

The last thing you want to have to worry about is going back to work after 10 years of retirement because you made a financial mistake. It's not fair to your friends and family members to place the burden of your questions on their shoulders. Instead make sure you find an expert who specializes in retirement planning. Ask your friends and family members the most important question of all, "Who is the best retirement expert in the world?" Seek them out and pay for their advice. It could be one of the smartest investments you ever make.

Chapter 8

LONG-TERM CARE INSURANCE— DO YOU REALLY NEED IT?

I never want to be a burden to my children
either physically or financially.

We hear this kind of statement over and over again, but when we bring up the topic of long-term care insurance, most people don't think they will ever need it. Those who do think they'll need it want to sit down with a planner and talk about the best way to plan for this potential event. Unfortunately, what they usually do is sit down with an insurance salesperson whose only goal is to sell a policy regardless of whether it is the right one for the individual person's situation.

So how do you plan for long-term care and should you consider long-term care insurance?

WHAT'S YOUR RISK?

A study by the U.S. Department of Health and Human Services [1]says people who reach age sixty-five will have a 52 percent

---

1   https://aspe.hhs.gov/basic-report/long-term-services-and-supports-older-americans-risks-and-financing-research-brief
https://longtermcare.acl.gov/the-basics/

chance of entering a nursing home. About 10 percent of the people who enter a nursing home will stay there five years or more. Even with these staggering statistics, most people don't believe this situation will ever happen to them.

They'll argue their parents never needed care, they eat well and exercise regularly, and they are absolutely opposed to the idea they could ever lose their independence. Frankly, who can blame them? If you woke up every morning thinking your future existence might be one of dependence and ill health, why would you want to get out of bed?

WHAT ARE THE COSTS OF CARE?

Below are the national medians for home care, assisted living, and nursing homes taken from the Genworth 2017 cost of care survey.[2]

- Home Health Aide = $4,099 per month = $49,188 per year

- Assisted Living = $3,750 per month = $45,000 per year

- Nursing Home = $8,121 per month = $97,452 per year

Keep in mind that these numbers are as 2017. Most of the people who are looking into this type of planning may not need care for 15 to 25 more years. So if the cost today is $8,121 per month, then the cost of care in 30 years will probably be closer to $19,138 per month assuming 3 percent inflation. You would have to come up with an additional $236,542 in annual income for 2.8 years to cover this amount.

2 https://www.genworth.com/about-us/industry-expertise/cost-of-care.html
   Accessed June 14, 2017.

LONG-TERM CARE INSURANCE

Long-term Care (LTC) Insurance is expensive (although less so if you purchase it while you are still young), and I believe that everyone should consider it. Early in my career, I was afraid to tell people they really needed to buy long-term care insurance. I didn't want to come across sounding like a pushy insurance salesperson. But life changes your opinions. I am now a very passionate advocate for long-term care insurance.

A good friend of mine, who was sixty years old at the time, was driving in his car when his driving became rather erratic. Some people called 911 to report a possible drunk driver. When the highway patrol arrived, they found my friend pulled off to the side of the road. He'd had a massive stroke. He has been on the road to recovery for several years and is now doing fairly well. However, he has lost most of his ability to move the right side of his body, and he has not regained his ability to speak yet. This friend had been in great health. He had been a vegetarian for more than thirty years. He worked out and meditated three days per week. He was the last person I would have ever thought would need long-term care, and because of his health, I never suggested or recommended he consider long-term care insurance.

A few years ago, a couple came to see me whom I asked whether they had long-term care insurance. They did not. I lightly suggested they consider looking into it. Two years went by, but they never followed up on getting any. Today, the wife has dementia, and they are paying a lot of money out of their retirement savings to help provide in-home care for her.

Unfortunately, when you specialize in working with retirees, you come across long-term care issues often. Because of these experiences, I have become a firm believer in long-term care insurance.

Some people are under the impression that they don't need to buy insurance. Their reasons are:

- The government will take care of me.

- My parents never needed long-term care.

- If I need care, my kids can take care of me.

- I exercise and eat right so I will never need long-term care.

- Long-term care insurance is too expensive.

- I will never go to a nursing home. I want to stay in my own home.

- I have enough money so I will self-insure against this risk.

Let's take a closer look at these reasons.

The government will take care of me.

A couple of years back, I read a report that Washington State's single biggest expense was the Department of Social and Health Services (DSHS). It was the first year that DSHS surpassed education as the State's biggest expense. DSHS and Medicaid is the federal and state welfare system that can help people pay for care. Remember this system is welfare. So you need to qualify based on your health and finances.

Your health has to be very bad, and your money has to be pretty much gone before you can qualify for this program. Some exceptions exist to this rule, so if you hire the right attorney, you may get around the "rules." Personally, I have ethical issues with that type of planning. Many people feel they are entitled to a government handout and will do anything possible to tweak the system so the burden of responsibility is shifted from the individual to the taxpayer. Don't get me wrong. I'm glad we have a safety net for those who need it, but it is not okay for people to abuse the system.

If you are healthy and can afford insurance premiums then please consider purchasing a good old fashioned private long-term care policy. I am of the opinion that you should always hope for the best, but plan for the worst.

My parents never needed long-term care.

Insurance companies are in business to make a profit. They are not going to offer insurance to people who already require care. They are not going to offer insurance to people who are likely to need care. Insurance companies have developed very sophisticated systems for evaluating your health and the risk of you needing care. They check your medical records and review all of the prescription medications you take. They do in-home health screening and phone interviews to check your cognitive ability. They are going to scrutinize your health thoroughly, and then they will only accept the healthiest people to reduce their risk of paying claims.

Insurance companies are very smart at reducing their exposure to this risk.

However, whether or not your parents needed LTC is not a major factor in evaluating you for risk. When you apply for life insurance, the companies want to know all about the life expectancy of your mom, dad, brothers, and sisters. In life insurance, a direct correlation between life expectancy and your heritage exists, but not with LTC insurance.

So maybe your folks needed care or maybe they didn't. Either way, that is not generally relevant to whether or not you may someday need it.

If I need care, my kids can take care of me.

Some people have children who are registered nurses and doctors, and they have an extra home on their property, so they plan for mom and dad to move in if they ever need care. Heck, why not? They love their parents. They have the care-giving expertise and a special home on their property just for this need. But that is not the case for most of us. In fact, most of us have a romanticized view of growing old.

You may even be thinking, "When I get old, I hope I can move in with my kids and spend my time playing with the grandkids, helping out with the dishes, and reading and gardening to my heart's content." But what happens when your health starts to fail? Do you really want to place a care-giving burden on your family?

Do you want your children to have to bathe you? Do you want your kids to help clean you after you go to the bathroom, or worse do you want them to have to clean up the sheets because you weren't able to make it to the bathroom? Do you want your kids to be up all night with you because of your dementia while you wander around the home and can't remember who your children are?

Is that the type of legacy you want to leave? Do you want to be remembered for the last three to ten years of your life as the decrepit old person who needed twenty-four-hour care, and to bring your children to tears when they remember about the care they provided? Or do you want to be remembered as the supportive caring parent who provided for and loved his or her children?

When asked, most kids say they plan to care for their parents should something happen. Most kids will even try to provide the care. But after months or years of having to lift dad out of bed, they develop back problems, not to mention anxiety and stress issues. You can't realistically expect your 125-pound daughter to move your 185 pounds. You need to consider the ability of the caregiver to do those everyday things, and how comfortable you'd be if your caregiver were a family member or a friend. My wife cared for her mom in this capacity for several months. While the children are very concerned and want the best for their parents, it's very difficult work physically and emotionally, even in the best situations. Being a caregiver by itself is hard enough, but caring for a person you love is even harder.

Please understand; care-giving is a burden you will be placing on your family in your time of need if you don't make other provisions.

When you own long-term care insurance, you and your family will have more options. Your children can still be involved in your care, but it can be on their terms, rather than their feeling obligated and stuck with no way out. I don't know about you, but I buy insurance to protect the people I love. I own life insurance to replace income and pay off debt if I die. I own disability insurance because if I can't work, I want my family to be able to buy groceries and meet our obligations. I own health insurance, car insurance, and homeowner's insurance because I want to protect my family from the loss associated with these items. Insurance is about protecting the people you love. Sure your kids can take care of you, but do you want them to?

I exercise and eat right so I will never need long-term care.

I believe taking care of your health will greatly reduce your likelihood of needing long-term care. I too eat right and exercise three times a week. I ran the Seattle marathon in 2002. I value good health and strive to make my health a priority in my life, but even though I am healthier than most people I know, I still own health insurance.

Long-term care insurance is an extension of health insurance. It just pays for a health issue after your regular health insurance will no longer pay for the ongoing care you may need. Eating right and exercising will likely increase your life expectancy. My hope is that taking these steps will help ward off your ever needing care. Heck, I wish no one ever needed long-term care. But the reality is that it happens to the best of us. It happens to the healthiest of us.

I have a client who developed dementia in his early eighties. He was a vibrant and healthy engineer. Dementia and Alzheimer's are ugly diseases that can strike even the healthiest people, and a host of other diseases may strike you regardless of how healthy you currently are. He had no idea he would develop dementia, and you don't know that you won't develop it as well. You should plan to be prepared for the possibilities you can't predict.

Long-term care insurance is too expensive.

One of the biggest misconceptions about long-term care insurance is that it's too expensive, but it is actually quite cheap when compared to the cost of actually needing care. If you are 60 years old and married, then a decent policy[3], today, for you and your wife combined, will cost between $5,500 and $7,200 per year for LTC insurance or between $2,750 and $3,600 per person per year for coverage. That may sound expensive compared to your homeowner's insurance, but when compared to the cost of long-term care, the insurance is a bargain.

According to the 2017 Genworth Cost of Care survey, the national median is $267 dollars per day in a nursing home with a private room. For a month, it would be $8,121, and for a year about $97,455. Those numbers are in today's dollars. The cost of care

---

3 Based on Washington State, shared coverage, $200/day, 3 percent compound inflation, 90 day elimination period, 3 years, 100% home healthcare as of June 15, 2017.

is only going to go up in the future, and it will likely double to $236,549 for facility care in 30 years.[4]

Which one would you rather pay: twenty years of premiums at $6,000 per year, or $21,145 per month for a total of $253,74. per year for the actual care? Medicare reports that once you turn age sixty-five, you have a 40 percent chance you will require some assistance before you die—that's a very high probability. The average length of time that care is needed is 2.8 years. Imagine you had a 40 percent probability your house would catch on fire. Would you go without homeowner's insurance? The chance of your home catching on fire is about 1 in 1,200. The chances of you needing long-term care are 2 in 5. Long-term care insurance will be more expensive to own than homeowner's insurance because it is much more likely to be needed so it is a more expensive risk to the insurance company.

I will never go to a nursing home. I want to stay in my own home.

Most people want to stay in their own homes as long as possible. My family had a family member who was in his mid-nineties when he finally needed care. We were having a hard time providing the care he needed in his home, so we thought he would be better off in a facility. We moved him to a facility, and were paying around $6,000 per month for a very nice private room. After a few less than desirable events, we decided to bring him home because we were not satisfied with the level of care he was receiving. To have the same level of around-the-clock nursing care at home cost us

4   https://www.genworth.com/about-us/industry-expertise/cost-of-care.html#

around $9,000 per month. Anything is possible, if you have the money to pay for it.

If you tour a nursing home and ask how many of the residents had planned to end up there, they will all tell you they never thought they would end up there. The good news is your options for your care are expanding. You could receive all of your care in the comfort of your home. Most insurance policies today will pay for care in either your home, in assisted living facilities, or in nursing homes. Just be sure when buying a policy that it will provide for you in your desired place.

I have enough money so I will self-insure the risk.

This excuse is probably the most ridiculous one we have ever heard. Buying long-term care insurance has nothing to do with whether you can pay for your care, and it has everything to do with denying you will ever need the care. If you have enough money to self-insure against the risk of long-term care, then you also have enough money to cancel your homeowner's insurance, knowing that if your home burns down, you could afford to pay for it out of your savings. Or you could cancel your health insurance because if you need major medical care, you could likely cover the cost.

Maybe you can afford to self-insure, but do you really want to risk the expense? You worked your entire life to accumulate what you have, so then, when it's all said and done, do you want to transfer all or a large portion of your wealth to a care facility? Every day you worked hard and saved while others spent like crazy so that one day you would have a large nest egg; do you really want to spend it all on old age care?

If you have enough money to self-insure, then it certainly makes sense to use a small portion of the interest you earn every year to protect the entire nest egg. It comes back to protecting the people who are important to you. If you don't have any family and don't have any church or organization that would benefit from your lifetime of hard work, then by all means please don't buy insurance. Just go ahead and write out the check to the nursing home today.

The good news is that the insurance companies have created combination products for people who don't want to "waste" their premium dollars on insurance they will never need. For example, a life insurance policy is now available that has a long-term care rider on it for an additional cost, so if you ever need long-term care, you can access the death benefit to help offset those costs. If you never need long-term care, then you know you didn't waste the premium dollars because your heirs will receive any remaining death benefit although you will not recover the fee you paid for the LTC rider.

An annuity is also available that helps provide leverage for those who want to self-insure. With this strategy, let's say for example you purchase an annuity and then you can choose an optional rider to give you up to double or triple your annuity income amount (depending on the additional options you purchase) for qualified health care costs. These riders typically pay for these costs for a certain period of time, usually up to five years. These annuities not only provide you with the potential for lifetime guaranteed income, but also allow you to increase that income as needed.

Generally, in my opinion, if you have less than $2 million in liquid assets, long-term care insurance makes good financial sense. We insure every other aspect of our lives and our health, but for some reason, we often overlook an event that has a 40 percent probability of happening. That's kind of silly if you think about it. Unfortunately, most people don't start thinking about or planning for long-term care insurance until one of two things happens: They start to see their health change, and think, "Oh, I better get some insurance just in case, or they start seeing a friend or a loved one go though the long-term care process. When you see someone go through this process, you feel the impact it has on a family. You get a little dose of reality and start to think, "Boy, I never want to put my family into that type of situation."

Long-term care insurance can be very hard to qualify for. You have to be very healthy to get coverage, so many times when people finally start thinking about long-term care insurance, they just aren't healthy enough to qualify for coverage. A woman once called me and said she was interested in speaking with someone who could help her decide whether long-term care insurance was appropriate. When she wasn't willing to come to the office, I asked whether I could make a trip out to her house. I explained to her that you have to be pretty healthy to qualify for coverage; she said she was very healthy. Health I have found, however, is relative. When I arrived at her home, she was hooked up to oxygen and was sitting in a wheelchair. But this woman considered herself pretty healthy when compared to her friends. Insurance companies will decline coverage for a lot less than being in a wheelchair and on oxygen. We have seen people declined for high blood pressure in combination with sleep apnea.

Long-term care insurance just makes good financial sense. So when should you buy it? You should buy it as soon as you can afford it without changing your lifestyle. The younger you are, the cheaper it is. If you can buy a policy in your early or mid-fifties, then that would be great. Often, people are still paying for their kids' colleges in their mid-fifties so, from a planning perspective, try to have a policy in force by the time you turn sixty. Another and probably more important consideration is your health. You have to be very healthy to qualify for long-term care insurance. Generally people don't get healthier as they get older, so the younger you are, the more likely you will qualify health wise.

If insurance is the way to go, which company should I choose?

Let's assume you have come to the conclusion that you don't want your family or friends to be your caregivers, and you realize the cost of care is high, but you don't want to pay for it out of your savings. You would rather transfer the risk to an insurance company. Let's also assume you are in pretty good health and you have the finances to be comfortably able to afford long-term care insurance premiums without changing your lifestyle. You are ready to shop for insurance.

Whatever you do, work with an independent agent. You want someone who can help you find the right policy for you. Find a company that is A-rated or better by AM Best. Make sure the company has been in the long-term care insurance industry for at least fifteen years. I suggest you find out how many lives it covers. I believe, at a minimum, you want a company that insures a minimum of 100,000 people and preferably 500,000 or more. Find out about price stability. Has the company ever increased premiums on its existing book of business, and if so, how many times has it done so? Finding a company that meets all the above criteria is getting harder and harder.

DESIGNING COVERAGE

Designing coverage will require you work with someone who is capable of listening to your concerns. You want to build a policy around your financial situation, not just buy a cookie cutter policy. A good agent will want to know details about your family, finances, and health so he or she can put together a policy to fit your objectives and protect your family.

Once you have your long-term care insurance in place, you may never need to use it—frankly, I hope you don't, but you can sleep well at night knowing that if the situation arises, you will be taken care of without being a burden on your family physically or financially.

Chapter 9

TAX PLANNING

The hardest thing in the world to understand is the income tax.
— Albert Einstein

IS YOUR IRA A TAX TIME BOMB?

Most of the people we serve tell us they don't mind paying their "fair share" of taxes, but then they follow up by saying, "but I'd prefer not to pay more than my fair share." I think the term "fair" is kind of funny. I've learned that taxes always seem fair as long as I'm not the one having to pay them. I remember my dad used to tell me, "Life is not fair, but it favors the prepared mind." I also recently read that "ignorance may be bliss, but it's expensive" and not planning or ignoring your future tax liability could create a future tax time bomb.

When I talk about retirement accounts, I am generally referring to accounts such as IRAs, 401(k)s, TSPs, and 403(b)s. These are accounts which you have contributed pre-tax dollars and those dollars are growing tax deferred, but when you begin taking money out of these accounts they will be 100 percent taxable as ordinary income and taxed at your effective income tax rate.

According to the **www.taxfoundation.org** the top marginal income tax rate in 1950 was 91 percent, by 1980 the top marginal income tax rate was 70 percent, and today the top marginal income tax rate is 37 percent.

According to the **www.USdebtclock.org** as of June 2017 our national debt was 19.94 trillion dollars and growing exponentially per year.

In a recent report from the Social Security board of trustee's they reported, "The combined assets of the Old-Age and Survivors Insurance, and Disability Insurance (OASDI) Trust Funds are projected to become depleted in 2034, unchanged from last year, with 77 percent of benefits still payable at that time." [1]

Is this economic world we live in sustainable? Can we continue to run deficits, increase our nations debt and provide medicare and health care for all AND make good on our promise of Social Security income to retiree's with 10,000 baby boomers retiring every day and yet at the same time maintain all time low marginal income tax rates?

If I had to make an educated guess about the future, then I'd say our current economic situation just doesn't seem sustainable. I'm not a betting man, but if I were I'd bet that taxes in the future are likely to increase for some people, and that benefits for some people will likely decrease.

When the "fair standard" is applied, the "some people" will likely be hard working Americans who have been responsible with their finances, those who have managed to save and live within their means and who have accumulated wealth and are deemed to have accumulated more than their "fair share".

1   http://www.ssa.gov/pressoffice/pr/trustee13-pr.html. Accessed February 6, 2014.

As you will see in this scenario converting an IRA to a Roth IRA can be a great opportunity for some.

When Mr. Jones came to see me, he and his wife were both sixty-five years old and enjoying their retirement. They were living comfortably on their retirement income, which was made up of both pensions and Social Security benefits. Mr. Jones had $500,000 dollars in his IRA, which he had no intention of ever using.

The primary purpose of the money was twofold: first, and foremost, if anything happened to Mr. Jones, he knew his wife would need the money to supplement her income because his pension would only pay her 55 percent; second, the purpose of the money was to leave it to his children.

Now Mr. Jones didn't realize when he turned seventy-and-a-half that the IRS was going to require him to start taking distributions from his IRA, the Required Minimum Distribution (RMD). Even though he didn't need the money, he was going to be required to pull money out.

Please note that the IRS can penalize up to 50 percent of your RMD if you don't take it every year. For example, if the IRS required you to take $40,000 dollars out of your retirement account the first year and you didn't, then it could impose a $20,000 penalty for that year.

So I asked Mr. Jones whether he had ever sat down to look at what the future tax liability might be on that IRA. We made some pretty conservative assumptions:

- Currently age sixty-five

- Assumed a 6 percent return annually on his investments

- He will take out his RMD every year and no extra

- Because of his family history and current health, we assume a life expectancy of age ninety.

PROJECTED IRA DISTRIBUTIONS							
	Age		Beginning	6.00 percent	RMD	Required	Ending
Year	Beg	End	Balance	Earnings	Divisor	Distribution	Balance
2009	64	65	$500,000	$30,000		$0	$530,000
2010	65	66	$530,000	$31,800		$0	$561,800
2011	66	67	$561,800	$33,708		$0	$595,508
2012	67	68	$595,508	$35,730		$0	$631,238
2013	68	69	$631,238	$37,874		$0	$669,113
2014	69	70	$669,113	$40,147	27.4	$24,420	$684,839
2015	70	71	$684,839	$41,090	26.5	$25,843	$700,087
2016	71	72	$700,087	$42,005	25.6	$27,347	$714,745
2017	72	73	$714,745	$42,885	24.7	$28,937	$728,692
2018	73	74	$728,692	$43,722	23.8	$30,617	$741,797
2019	74	75	$741,797	$44,508	22.9	$32,393	$753,912
2020	75	76	$753,912	$45,235	22.0	$34,269	$764,878
2021	76	77	$764,878	$45,893	21.2	$36,079	$774,691
2022	77	78	$774,691	$46,481	20.3	$38,162	$783,010
2023	78	79	$783,010	$46,981	19.5	$40,154	$789,837
2024	79	80	$789,837	$47,390	18.7	$42,237	$794,990
2025	80	81	$794,990	$47,699	17.9	$44,413	$798,276
2026	81	82	$798,276	$47,897	17.1	$46,683	$799,490
2027	82	83	$799,490	$47,969	16.3	$49,048	$798,411
2028	83	84	$798,411	$47,905	15.5	$51,510	$794,805
2029	84	85	$794,805	$47,688	14.8	$53,703	$788,790
2030	85	86	$788,790	$47,327	14.1	$55,943	$780,175
2031	86	87	$780,175	$46,811	13.4	$58,222	$768,764
2032	87	88	$768,764	$46,126	12.7	$60,533	$754,357
2033	88	89	$754,357	$45,261	12.0	$62,863	$736,755
2034	89	90	$736,755	$44,205	11.4	$64,628	$716,333

Total RMDs: $908,005

Total Taxed: **$1,624,338**

Hypothetical only - no specific investment illustrated.

Mr. Jones, over his life expectancy, could end up taking $900,000 dollars out of his IRA in RMDs. Remember, he doesn't want to take anything out, but he is required to by the IRS. When he dies, his IRA will still have $700,000 in it.

Now, assuming the worst case scenario, all of the money at this point transfers to his named beneficiary who chooses to take a lump sum distribution instead of stretching it out over his lifetime; then he would have total taxable distributions of $1.6 million.

Think about that for a minute. Today, Mr. Jones starts with $500,000, and upon his death, he will end up with $1.6 million of taxable distributions from his account.

We currently have some of the lowest marginal income tax rates in our country's history. So let's pretend that taxes aren't going to go up and we will be able to maintain these ultra low tax rates for the next twenty-five years. It seems a bit ridiculous to me to make this assumption given the amount of spending our government is doing, but let's pretend the tax rates will stay low to keep the math easy. If we assume Mr. Jones pays 25 percent tax on his $1.6 million of taxable distribution, he would be looking at a prolonged and future tax liability of $400,000.

The question every person in our country should be asking is: "If I could protect my retirement account from excessive taxation, would I want to? Is there a better way?"

Maybe. It depends on how you plan to use your money and what's most important to you. But if you want to give Uncle Sam as little of your hard-earned money as possible, wouldn't you want to know how to do it?

Depending on how we choose to fix this problem, we can reduce that tax liability. Not only can we reduce a person's tax liability, but we can also structure his accounts so when he turns seventy-and-a-half, he won't be required to take any money out.

This structuring gives a person the ability to allow that account to compound and grow income tax free for decades. Imagine, tax free not just for his life, but also for the income his wife may need, and, if done properly, it could mean a lifetime of tax free distributions to his children for years and years and years. I don't know of anyone who wants to pay Uncle Sam more than he should, but how many of you would know whether or not you are?

Remember that tax preparation is different than tax planning. Keep in mind it's not how much you make—it's how much you keep.

IMPORTANT LINES ON YOUR TAX RETURN

Well, last year is behind us, and what is done, is done with respect to your annual income tax return. If you are retired, you should review these important line items on your 1040 tax return and make sure you understand how they impact your financial life. Get out your income tax return and circle the following:

Line 8a	Line 9a	Line9b	Line 13
Line 20b	Line 40	Line 43	

Someone once taught me, "it's not about how much money you make, but rather how much money you keep." I've also learned that retirement is all about cash flow, not net worth, and to make sure that your cash flow is as tax efficient as possible.

You may have income you receive, but don't spend, and that income could be costing you thousands of dollars every year in unnecessary taxation.

Now you are probably thinking, "We spend all of our income." If so, then that's great. But often many retirees have income that causes them to pay more money in taxes. They are not necessarily using the income for every day living expenses.

Question #1: When looking at your tax return, is there a number listed in line 8a, line 9a or line 9b?

Question #2: Are you spending that income?

For example, if you have a certificate of deposit in a non-qualified account that is paying you interest, and you are reinvesting the interest rather than spending it, then at the end of the year you would get a 1099 from your bank. You will pay taxes on the interest income you received regardless of whether or not you spent it.

But even more important than the tax you pay on your interest, is understanding how it impacts the rest of your tax return. The interest income will be used in the calculation for determining what percentage of your Social Security benefits will be taxed, which can be as little as 0 percent or as much as 85 percent of your Social Security benefits.

These additional income sources flow through your return and as a result could impact how much of your itemized deductions can be captured.

If you are one of those big hearted people that would like to pay more money to our Government every year to help pay down our national debt, check out this website to learn how you can give a little extra of your hard earned money to Uncle Sam. ;-) Help pay down our National Debt by visiting: **www.treasurydirect.gov/govt/reports/pd/gift/gift.htm.**

Chapter 10

THE IRA LEGACY OPTIMIZER

REQUIRED MINIMUM DISTRIBUTIONS

Most people know that once you reach age 70.5 the IRS requires you to begin taking distributions from your IRA (Individual Retirement Arrangements.) What most people don't realize is if you do not take the required minimum distribution (RMD) in a timely fashion every year you could face a 50 percent penalty. Let's say you had one million dollars in your IRA, then your required minimum distribution the year you turn 70.5 would be approximately $36,496. If you failed to take the distribution, then the penalty would be $18,248. This is one of the steeper penalties I've ever encountered in the tax code. Be sure to make yourself a reminder on your calendar to take your distribution every year.

To calculate how much you need to take from your IRA you might want to visit the IRS website or consult a tax adviser. It would also be a good idea to review publication 590 to see which table you need to use for determining your withdrawal.[1]

1   http://www.irs.gov/publications/p590/ar02.html. Accessed February 6, 2014.

Most of the people we have worked with over the years seem to use Table 3, which can be found at **www.irs.gov** by doing a quick search on RMDs.

People who use this table are either unmarried owners, married owners whose spouse is not more than 10 years younger, or married owners whose spouses are not the sole beneficiary of their IRA.

To calculate your IRA Minimum Required Withdrawal you would take the value of your IRA from December 31st of the prior year and divide it by the distribution period taken from the uniform life time table. For example: your IRA had a $100,000 balance on December 31st last year, and you are currently 71 years old. You would determine your IRA RMD by dividing $100,000 by a distribution period of 26.5, and you would need to take a distribution of $3,773.59.

A question we are often asked is, "What percentage do I need to withdrawal from my IRA to meet the required minimum distribution." In the example above, we show you the correct way for determining your required minimum withdrawal, but just to satisfy our curiosity we backed into the numbers to show approximately what percentage you would have to withdrawal to equal the correct withdrawal rate. We are including the chart showing the percentages below merely as an interesting side note, and *you should not use these numbers for calculating your required minimum withdrawal from your individual retirement account.*

Age	Distribution Percentage	Age	Distribution Percentage
70	3.6496350%	93	10.4166667%
71	3.7735849%	94	10.9890110%
72	3.9062500%	95	11.6279070%
73	4.0485830%	96	12.3456790%
74	4.2016807%	97	13.1578947%
75	4.3668122%	98	14.0845070%
76	4.5454545%	99	14.9253731%
77	4.7169811%	100	15.8730159%
78	4.9261084%	101	16.9491525%
79	5.1282051%	102	18.1818182%
80	5.3475936%	103	19.2307692%
81	5.5865922%	104	20.4081633%
82	5.8479532%	105	22.2222222%
83	6.1349693%	106	23.8095238%
84	6.4516129%	107	25.6410256%
85	6.7567568%	108	27.0270270%
86	7.0921986%	109	29.4117647%
87	7.4626866%	110	32.2580645%
88	7.8740157%	111	34.4827586%
89	8.3333333%	112	38.4615385%
90	8.7719298%	113	41.6666667%
91	9.2592593%	114	47.6190476%
92	9.8039216%	115 & over	52.6315789%

FINRA, the financial industry regulatory authority created a handy little required minimum distribution calculator, which you can check out by visiting **http://apps.finra.org/Calcs/1/RMD**.

As always be sure to get expert advice before taking a distribution to satisfy your RMD. I'd hate to see you end up with a 50 percent penalty. This information was written as of June 2017 and it is possible that the information may change. So again please consult the IRS publication 590 and a qualified tax adviser before taking action.

We meet a lot of people today who tell us they live comfortably on their pension and their Social Security. Oftentimes, these folks have a sizeable amount of money in their IRA accounts, and that money's purpose is to pay for emergencies, occasional travel, putting a new roof on the house, or potentially buying a new car. These people have generally named their spouses as their beneficiaries and their children as their contingent beneficiaries, and most have never pulled money out of these accounts. So even though people are planning to use these tax deferred savings accounts as emergency funds, the reality is that they aren't being used at all. Why should that matter?

The IRS says that at age 70 1/2, you are required to begin taking distributions from your IRA. This does not apply to a Roth IRA. When people take this distribution, if they don't need the money for living expenses, they will often reinvest it in either a taxable investment account or certificates of deposit at the bank. Either way, they are creating an additional tax liability.

When you take your Required Minimum Distribution, you are taxed at your ordinary income tax rate, which is generally your highest rate as well. You then take the after-tax dollars and deposit them into your CDs at the bank. At the end of the year, you will receive a 1099 for the interest income earned on your CD. Even if you don't use the money and just reinvest it, you have to pay tax on the interest income.

Some people don't like the idea of using either savings bonds or tax-deferred fixed rate annuities to defer the interest income into the future because they believe taxes will likely go up, and they would rather pay tax rates at today's all-time low marginal rates, which makes sense. But an often overlooked opportunity exists. The money from your RMD can fund a life insurance policy.

That is why Albert Einstein said, "The most powerful force in the universe is compound interest." Remember, your IRA is probably your most tax-hostile money. Every dollar you pull out of your IRA is going to be taxed at your ordinary effective income tax bracket (normally the highest). People say, "Yeah, but when I am retired, I'll be in a lower tax bracket." Do you really believe that?

In 2017, the Tax Cuts and Jobs Act was passed, which lowered marginal income tax rates to historically low levels. The U.S. Government is spending money like crazy. Ten thousand baby boomers are retiring every single day and putting pressure on programs like Medicare and Social Security, which are already strained. And you, in your heart of hearts, believe taxes are going to stay at these all time low levels?

CALCULATE THE GROSS DISTRIBUTION TO FIND THE NET AFTER-TAX SUM

I see a lot of people miscalculate their gross distribution from their IRAs when they have a specific net /after-tax amount they need.

For example, you want to take a net/after-tax distribution of $5,000 from your IRA, and you are in the 28 percent tax bracket. You want to calculate how much your gross distribution should be so that you end up with a net/after-tax distribution of $5,000.

- A 28 percent tax would be represented in decimals as 0.28.

- First subtract 1 -(minus) 0.28 on your calculator and you get = 0.72

- Take the net distribution you would like so in this case $5,000 and divide it by 0.72 = $6,944.44

So if you take a distribution from your IRA for $6,944 and have 28 percent or $1,944.32 withheld for taxes, you would net $5,000 after-tax from your IRA.

- $6,944 was the gross distribution
  -$1,944.32 was the 28 percent tax withholding

  _____

  = $5,000 Net IRA distribution after tax

- Here is the formula for this scenario:
  1-0.28 = 0.72
  $5,000/0.72 = $6,944.44

- 1 - tax bracket converted to a decimal = X
  Net distribution/X = gross distribution.

A lot of people start with the net distribution ($5,000 in this example) and multiply it by the tax rate (28 percent in the example). If you do this you get $1,400. They then add the $1,400 plus the $5,000 to come up with $6,400. The problem is if you request a gross distribution of $6,400 multiplied by 28 percent it equals $1,792, and you end up with a net distribution of $4,608 which was not the desired outcome.

QUALIFIED CHARITABLE DISTRIBUTIONS (QCD) ARE NOW PERMANENT: SHOULD YOU GIVE TO A CHARITY FROM AN IRA

In 2015 Congress voted to make the Qualified Charitable Distributions a permanent part of the tax code. President Obama signed the bill on December 18, 2015. This means you no longer have to wait on Congress for a last minute deal to plan your charitable contributions from an IRA.

When you give a Qualified Charitable Distribution (QCD) directly to a charity from your IRA, you may save more in taxes than you realize.

Now that congress has made the QCD permanent, the law allows people who are 70 1/2, who must take a required minimum distribution (RMD), to exclude up to $100,000 from gross income for donations paid directly to a qualified charity from their IRA. This is powerful because the gift satisfies the RMD and is not included as taxable income on your tax return.

When you reduce the amount of income that hits the front page of your tax return, it filters through other calculations such as the provisional income rules that determine how much of your social security is taxable and ultimately impacts your adjusted gross income.

We know a lot of people who give to their church and other charities on a regular basis. Why not get the very most tax benefit out of those gifts?

Most people do not mind paying their fair share in taxes, but most people do not want to pay more than their fair share in taxes. By using the Qualified Charitable Distributions to satisfy your charitable giving and your required minimum distribution it may help you pay less money in taxes and continue a legacy of stewardship.

Here are a few key points to remember:

- Assets must be transferred directly from an IRA to a Charity.

- Donations must be made before December 31st.

- You cannot give to donor-advised funds, charitable annuities or a grant making foundations.

- As the IRA owner you are responsible for having proof of the gift before filing your tax return.

- Married individuals filing a joint return could exclude up to $100,000 from each of the spouses own IRA's.

- The amount excluded from gross income is not deductible.

- For higher income medicare beneficiaries making a contribution from your IRA directly to a charity may also help you avoid having to pay income related monthly adjusted amount (IRMAA) which is an extra charge added to your premiums for Medicare Part B and Part D.

Please consult with your CPA or tax adviser before taking any action on anything discussed.

Here is the IRS website for more information on qualified charitable contributions.

https://www.irs.gov/Retirement-Plans/Charitable-Donations-from-IRAs

https://www.irs.gov/Charities-&-Non-Profits/Exempt-Organizations-Select-Check

Chapter 11

PAYING OFF DEBT VS. SUPERSIZING YOUR RETIREMENT INCOME

When my son Oliver was just about two years old, we lived in a two-story home where our stairs went down about three steps, came to a platform, turned, went down another seven steps, hit another platform, turned and then went down the final three steps. I would stand on the first platform and Oliver would run and jump to me, flying over the three steps, and I would catch him. He would laugh, I would laugh, and I would swing him around and give him a big hug.

Then one day I was carrying some laundry down the steps in the dark. I had just stepped down onto that first platform when all of a sudden I heard the pitter patter of little feet running in the dark. I turned around just as Oliver took flight. I dropped all of the clothes and did my best to catch him. Somehow, he managed to fly past the first platform and was on his way down the longer flight of steps. I grabbed him by the ankle and we both ended up lying face first, facing down the stairs. Of course, he was crying, but fortunately, he wasn't hurt. We were both very scared. My heart was pounding as I held him. I felt so bad.

The next day I stood on that platform and looked at him. He got a little sparkle in his eye and started to run toward me, but just before it was time to jump, he stopped. It's a horrible feeling to have started a game that resulted in my son falling down the stairs. It's an even more horrible feeling to have had a relationship where there was 100 percent trust and to see that trust damaged because of my mistake.

I do the best financial planning I can for my clients, but despite my best efforts, sometimes things don't go as planned. The sinking sensation in my gut when I dropped my son is the same feeling I get when I see people receiving bad advice, or when I make an error in assessing a situation.

THE RISK OF PAYING OFF DEBT

Getting out of debt is incredibly smart and not using credit is brilliant. But does it ever not make sense to pay off debt?

Let's take a look at an example when paying off debt may not make sense. Let's assume the following:

- A married couple who are both 70 years old

- They have a 30-year mortgage of $130,000 with a fairly large mortgage payment at 4.75 percent, paying an additional $300 per month to pay it off early

- $150,000 in savings

- Not enough income to live comfortably every month

Remember, retirement is all about cash flow, not net worth. While I am certainly a proponent of being debt-free, it doesn't make sense for this couple to make these extra payments toward their principal. An extra couple of hundred dollars a month could really make a significant impact on their existing lifestyle.

Should you try your hardest to get your debt paid off? Absolutely, but don't do it at the cost of your retirement years. I know it's wonderful not to have any debt, and I hope by the time you are retired, you don't have this concern. But is it worth making extreme sacrifices that won't likely benefit you? No.

Let me give you another example of how paying off your debt can hurt your retirement. Let's assume these particular folks are both 86, have grown children, and have done everything they can to be financially responsible by staying out of debt. When they retired at age 70, they used their $100,000 savings to pay off their $80,000 mortgage and are living off their social security checks.

So now it's 16 years later, and their car that is twenty years old is in need of a lot of repair. They only have a $20,000 nest egg left over after paying off their mortgage, and had gradually spent that down between a few small trips, miscellaneous home and car repairs, and the increasing cost of living. They're now 86 years old with no debt, and unfortunately, not enough income. They can barely survive, let alone achieve clarity, confidence and freedom. So what could they do now?

Have you ever heard the saying "different strokes for different folks?" Retirement planning is never a "one size fits all" and what works wonderfully for some folks is absolutely the wrong concept for others.

One option to consider is selling your home or taking out a reverse mortgage on your home. I know many people initially recoil from the idea of a reverse mortgage, but it can creatively solve financial issues for certain people. Let me give you another example of how it could help.

HOME EQUITY CONVERSION MORTGAGE (HECM)

Let's look at a hypothetical example of how a home equity conversion mortgage (HECM) could be used to help you increase your retirement income and be sure to leave a legacy to your heirs. Let's assume Mr. Moon is 70 and Mrs. Moon is 68 years old. They are in very good health and have been retired for almost fifteen years. When they retired, their pension was more than enough to cover all of their living expenses. During the last 15 years, they have seen their medical costs rise substantially, their property taxes increase, and the cost of living increase, which has eaten away at their modest retirement savings. So now they are feeling an income pinch. Mr. Moon is considering going back to work, and they have been taking aggressive steps to cut their expenses. In fact, they are driving a car that is twenty years old, they have canceled their cable television, and they are considering not taking all of their prescriptions to try and save a few extra dollars.

Before Mr. and Mrs. Moon retired, they had paid off their home. Their home is by far their largest asset, and if they had to sell it today, they could probably sell it for $300,000. They think selling their home would free up the capital they would need to live more comfortably. So they start looking to downsize. Unfortunately, what they find is that even the smaller decent homes in nice neighborhoods are going for around $300,000, so they will only break even. They do not want to move into an apartment; in fact, they don't want to move at all. They have lived in the same home for more than thirty years, and they have a lot of wonderful memories, an incredible garden, great neighbors, and they are comfortable. They also know that although they love their home, their children are not interested in owning it after they die. More than likely, their children will sell the house and split the proceeds from it.

If I was their financial adviser, I would have asked them whether they had ever considered using a HECM. However, one of their first questions would probably be, "If we use a HECM, then would we still be able to leave anything to our children?" which is an important question. So how much would they want to leave to their kids? For this scenario let's assume $100,000 each.

Based on the above, by using a HECM they would have been able to generate a guaranteed income stream of $1,000 per month for the rest of their lives as long as they lived in their home. From that $1,000, we could use $300 to buy a second-to-die guaranteed universal life insurance contract that would pay an income-tax-free death benefit of $200,000 upon the death of the second spouse with each child listed as a beneficiary at 50 percent each or $100,000 for each of their two children. The guaranteed death benefit would be to age 110, so it is highly unlikely they would outlive the insurance contract. This leaves them with $700 per month to make ends meet.

Now as with any planning, advantages and disadvantages exist, and you should consider all of the different what-ifs, costs, and risks. While this type of planning is certainly not appropriate for everyone, it would obviously accomplished the desired goals for Mr. and Mrs. Moon and might also be an option for the other couple who had paid off their home and are now are at risk of losing their retirement lifestyle due to lack of retirement income.

Chapter 12

HEALTH CARE INSURANCE BEFORE & AFTER RETIREMENT

As you head into and through retirement, one of the most important aspects of your financial security will be your health insurance plan. It can affect the age at which you decide to retire and can also be one of your largest retirement expenses.

An article from Fidelity Investments recently caught my eye. Its title was "Retiree health costs rise: A couple may need to spend almost $275,000 on health care in retirement. Planning is key." That dollar figure may sound high but, with modern medicine, people are generally living longer than their ancestors. It is not unrealistic to think of your life as divided into three phases: birth to age 30, ages 31 to 60, and ages 61 to 90. Viewed this way, it is easy to see that you may spend up to one-third of your life in retirement. The article goes on to explain that if you are not factoring health care costs into retirement planning, you could face a future unpleasant shock.

Not long ago, I met with a couple who retired in their late 50s and did not fully research and understand the cost of health insurance before retiring. Many people are used to having insurance through their employer. They are not aware of the cost of individual health insurance and the process of applying for insurance through health care exchanges available since the passage of the Affordable Care Act (also known as Obamacare) in 2010. Currently, a married couple in their late 50s in Kitsap County, Washington, could be looking at monthly premiums for a health care plan starting at $920 per month, with an $8,000 family deductible per year. With lower deductibles, the premiums would increase.

Federal health insurance premium tax subsidies or credits may help reduce your out-of-pocket insurance premiums when you purchase the insurance through the government health care exchange. For example, the couple above may be eligible for a health insurance premium tax credit based on their modified adjusted gross income (MAGI). If their MAGI for the year was $55,000, they could receive a $704 per month tax credit toward their premiums, and their out-of-pocket insurance premium would then be reduced to $216 per month. However, if their MAGI was $63,000, then they would have to shoulder the entire $920 per month, since they would not eligible for any of those tax credits. As you can see, the rules and regulations regarding health insurance are complex and vary depending upon your individual situation.

Health care costs are increasing due to longer life expectancies for individuals and annual increases for medical and prescription drug expenses, as well as an increase in more people using health care services. Of course, your specific medical costs in retirement will vary depending on your health and the choices you make about how to fund your health care costs. However, another critical factor is the age at which you retire. Many people don't have a choice about when to retire. Their health or a mandatory retirement age, such as a maximum age of 65 for some commercial airline pilots, may determine their retirement date. Regardless of your situation, however, health care costs should be an important consideration in your retirement planning.

In this chapter, we will share ideas and strategies to assist you in navigating today's complex health care field. Our goal is to help your achieve clarity, confidence, and freedom that you have made the right choices for yourself and your family as you prepare for and transition through retirement. The health care options available to you when you are younger than age 65 differ greatly from those available when you turn 65 and become eligible for Medicare. So, in this chapter, we will discuss these options separately.

HEALTH CARE OPTIONS BEFORE AGE 65

Many people have the opportunity to participate in an employer-sponsored health care plan or other group insurance plan while they are working. With these plans, your employer pays a portion of your health care premium costs, or the costs are shared among a pool of insured individuals. In the past, those who did not have access to such employer or group plans used to contact private insurance companies to find health coverage for themselves and their families. Not only was private insurance generally more expensive than employee/group plans, but pre-existing health problems often prevented these individuals from obtaining any health coverage or finding a comprehensive policy with reasonable premiums.

THE AFFORDABLE CARE ACT OF 2010

Under the Affordable Care Act, individuals who do not participate in an employer-sponsored or group health care plan, or who plan to retire early and will lose their employer-sponsored plan, are eligible to purchase private insurance or to enroll in health care coverage through a health care exchange. Depending on where you live, you may use the federal exchange available online at www.healthcare.gov or your own state health care exchange.

So, if you do not have an employer-sponsored or group health care plan, or if you plan to retire before you become age 65 and will lose your employer-sponsored plan, you have the option to participate in a health care exchange until you hit Medicare age or to buy your own insurance through an independent insurance agent.

COBRA HEALTH CARE PLANS

If you have an employer-sponsored health care plan and lose that health insurance coverage through a life event, you may be offered a COBRA insurance policy by your employer. Depending on your circumstances, COBRA may be available for 18 to 36 months after you've lost your employer-sponsored coverage. Not only can COBRA be an option for early retirement. It can also be an alternative during a job change, loss of a job, a reduction in work hours, a divorce, or the death of a person who carried the health insurance. COBRA stands for the Consolidated Omnibus Budget Reconciliation Act. This act was enacted into law in 1986 to help workers and their families continue to have health coverage during certain life events. It also gives workers who lose their health benefits the right to choose to continue group health benefits, for a certain set period of time, under certain circumstances.

Many people who retire early, say in their late 50s or early 60s and who are not yet eligible for Medicare, are looking to fill in a health insurance gap until they turn 65. I'll tell you, insurance premiums for people between the ages of about 58 to 65 are pretty steep. We see many folks who retire early, receive a COBRA offer from their employer, accept it without checking alternatives, and then later jump off COBRA and into an individual plan because it has better coverage or is less expensive. I urge you to have a qualified health insurance agent examine your employer COBRA offering beforehand, determine what is available on the private market, and help you make the best decision. Examining your health care options and determining if a COBRA plan is the right option for you should begin several months or a year before you retire.

One option to keep your insurance premiums down is to increase your deductible. If you are healthy, don't go to the doctor very often, and don't take many prescription drugs you may be able to take on the risk of having perhaps a $10,000 healthcare deductible.

HEALTH SAVINGS ACCOUNTS

If you have a high-deductible health care plan, prior to enrolling in Medicare, consider a Health Savings Account (HSA). The funds in an HSA can be used to pay medical expenses such as deductibles, co-pays, and other qualified out-of-pocket medical costs. The tax advantages of an HSA are that the funds contributed to the account are not subject to federal income tax at the time they are deposited. Similar to contributing to an Individual Retirement Account (IRA), you get a tax deduction for the funds you contribute annually to an HSA. Money in an HSA not spent for qualified medical expenses during the year can also be rolled over into future years, where it continues to accumulate tax free. A great advantage of an HSA, however, is that unlike an IRA, when you do spend the HSA funds for qualified medical expenses, you pay no taxes on the amount of money you withdraw from the account.

The federal government imposes limits on how much money can be contributed to an HSA annually for an individual or a family. In 2018, this limit was $3,450 per individual and $6,850 per family. If you have not had an HSA previously and are aged 55 and older, you may also be able to make "catch-up" contributions to help establish an HSA. In 2018, however, the amount for catch-up contributions was $1,000 annually. Once you turn age 65 and start Medicare, you can no longer contribute to an HSA.

I know many people who treat an HSA like another retirement account—but a retirement account that is set aside specifically for future health care costs. They may try to maximize their contributions to fund a 401K retirement plan and an IRA. But they may also have an HSA account. Even though they may have some medical expenses now, they choose not to use the HSA. They just let the funds in the account grow and earn compounded interest. Then, when they are older and withdraw funds to pay for health expenses, the money comes out tax-free. HSA funds taken out for non-qualified health care expenses will be subject to ordinary income taxes and potentially a 10 percent federal penalty too.

Some HSA accounts even allow you to invest the money. For example, I have an HSA that allows investment in several mutual funds rather than just sitting in a savings account earning almost nothing in today's interest rate environment.

ALTERNATIVE HEALTH CARE FUNDING

After passage of the Affordable Care Act in 2010, some individuals experienced difficulty using online health insurance exchanges, and some received notice that their insurance plans had been canceled. As a result, interest in alternative methods of funding health care expenses has grown rapidly. One such option is a non-insurance approach known as Health Care Sharing Ministries. These programs are offered by faith-based non-profit organizations that pool members' money to share medical expenses. Under the Affordable Care Act, these ministries are granted an exemption from the individual mandate, which means that participants who use this type of health care cost sharing do not incur an IRS tax penalty for not having health insurance. To learn more, visit **www.soundretirementplanning.com/category/radio/** and search for the word "alternative" in the "search my blog" box with the magnifying glass icon to find the interviews regarding Samaritan Ministries and Medi-Share.

HEALTH CARE OPTIONS AGE 65 AND OLDER

By the time you approach age 65, you have probably spent decades working and trying to save as much money as you can for your retirement. You may be thinking of doing all that traveling you've been dreaming of or having the funds to finally pursue projects you have been putting off for years. You probably didn't plan to spend much of your hard-earned money on health care expenses. For many people, however, that is a reality in their "golden years."

At the beginning of this chapter, we shared a statement from Fidelity Investments that an average couple could expect to spend nearly $275,000 on medical expenses in retirement. When I talk with my clients who are retired, they often tell me that their activities are planned around doctor appointments and other medical issues and that the costs add up quickly.

When you are retired and no longer working, your income is usually finite and comes from Social Security, savings, and investments. Most of us will have to control our fixed monthly expenses and discretionary spending in retirement to ensure that these funds will carry us through the rest of our lives. If you are working after age 65 and are still enrolled in an employer-sponsored health care plan, your choices will be different. In either case, making the right health care decisions are crucial to your financial well-being.

MEDICARE INSURANCE

For most people, the first Medicare event they encounter is pretty simple. A few months before your 65th birthday, you should receive notification in the mail that you are eligible to enroll in Medicare. If you are not working at age 65, it is essential that you enroll. You have a seven-month period to do so: three months before your 65th birthday month, during your birthday month, and 3 months afterward. If you do not do enroll during this time period, you may pay a penalty for the rest of your life, based on the number of months you wait beyond when you should have enrolled!

If you are still working at age 65, special rules apply. You usually don't need to sign up, unless you want to, until within 8 months after you leave your job. However, it pays to check with SSA to be sure. When you approach age 65, it is imperative that you answer three questions: (1) Must you enroll in Medicare? (2) Will you have a penalty if you do not enroll at age 65? and (3) What will your monthly Medicare premium be?

The answers to the above questions can greatly impact your health care costs throughout your retirement years. It is to your benefit to get some professional help with your Medicare decisions from a health insurance agent. You can also get personalized health insurance counseling at no cost from your local State Health Insurance Assistance Program (SHIP). You can find the SHIP in your state at www.shiptacenter.org. The website and the Medicare site at www.medicare.gov/your-medicare-costs/help-paying-costs/get-help-paying-costs.html will provide information to help you pay for health your insurance costs and learn if you are eligible for any insurance subsidies.

It is important to understand that not all medical services, items, and costs are covered by Medicare. Like all health insurance plans, Medicare has guidelines about what services and items will be paid for and in what dollar amount. You also have co-pays, deductibles, prescriptions, and other out-of-pocket expenses to pay while you are on Medicare. So, it is good to get a supplemental health insurance plan, sometimes referred to as a Medi-Gap health insurance policy to cover medical expenses not paid by Medicare. Even if you have a supplemental plan, that supplemental insurance will not cover all your expenses either. You will still have deductibles, co-pays, and non-covered services you will have to fund out of your retirement savings.

For example, generally Medicare will not cover most dental care, eye examinations related to prescribing glasses, dentures, cosmetic surgery, acupuncture, hearing aids and exams for fitting them, routine foot care, or long-term care. You will have to pay for the services, items, and costs Medicare does not cover, unless you have a supplemental insurance plan such as a private Medi-Gap plan or a special Medicare health plan that includes such coverage. One type of special Medicare health plan is a Medicare Advantage plan, which we discuss in Medicare Part C below. Regardless of the type of plan you choose, a couple 65 years of age can expect to pay about $9,000 annually for Medicare Parts A, B, D, and supplemental insurance.

Medicare has a Part A, Part B, Part C, and Part D, and each part offers different services. Sometimes I want to give the insurance program a Part F for complexity because it is not an easy system to navigate. So, let's summarize the different parts of Medicare to help you understand your choices.

MEDICARE PART A: HOSPITAL AND HOSPICE SERVICES

Medicare Part A is hospital insurance that covers inpatient hospital care, skilled nursing facility care, hospice, and in-facility lab tests and surgery, as well as home health care. Most people who have worked or whose spouse has worked don't pay any premiums for this part of the program. You have already paid for this part of Medicare as a portion of the FICA/Social Security premiums deducted from your pay checks as part of your payroll taxes when you were employed. You are automatically enrolled in Medicare Part A when you sign up for Social Security at age 65.

MEDICARE PART B: MEDICAL SERVICES

Medicare Part B covers medically necessary services needed to diagnose or treat a medical condition such as doctor visits, lab tests, and supplies like wheelchairs and walkers. Some services may be covered only in certain settings or for patients with certain conditions. Part B also covers preventive service to prevent illness or to detect it at an early stage, when treatment is most likely to work best. You pay a monthly premium for Part B—currently $134 a month or more. You should expect your Medicare premiums to increase every year by a few dollars.

MEDICARE PART C: MEDICARE ADVANTAGE PLANS

Medicare Part C is not a separate Medicare benefit. Part C refers to Medicare Advantage Plans, which combine your benefits from Medicare Parts A, B, and sometimes D (prescription drugs) into a single plan.

Medicare Advantage Plans are like one-stop shopping. They are private insurance plans, approved by Medicare, that combine your benefits from Medicare Parts A, B, and sometimes D (prescription drugs) and a supplemental insurance (or Medi-Gap) plan, into one plan for one price. You pay your Medicare Part B payment directly to Medicare. Or, if you are also enrolled in Social Security, your Medicare Part B is deducted from your Social Security payment and sent directly to Medicare (remember that most people pay no premium for Medicare Part A). Then your Medicare Part D and supplemental insurance are combined into an additional premium that you pay to the private Medicare Advantage insurance company. Even though you are paying separate premiums to Medicare and the private insurance company, the Medicare Advantage Plan manages all your health care coverage. They coordinate your Medicare Part A, B, D, and supplemental insurance, and you do not receive separate bills from Medicare for co-pays and deductibles—everything is funneled through the Medicare Advantage Plan, and you are billed through them.

MEDICARE PART D: PRESCRIPTION DRUG SERVICES

Medicare Part D covers prescription drug costs. You must pay for it, but it is optional. Part D is provided only through private insurance companies that have a contract with the government; it is not provided by the federal government itself. You don't have to buy it, but drug costs have soared in recent years, and it is a good idea to have such coverage, especially if you think your drug costs may increase in the future. Many people over age 65 find that prescription drugs are a major medical expense for them, even if they did not take any regular prescription drugs when they were younger.

Although you may have a Medicare Part D prescription drug plan, you could still have large out-of-pocket drug expenses if you must take specialty drugs. Many times, with these specialty medications, your Medicare Part D plan may pay only a percentage of the cost, and you still have to pay 30% to 50% of the cost of those expensive drugs. So, you must keep that fact in mind when planning for retirement and estimating your health care expenses.

To enroll in Medicare Part D, you can search for Medicare Part D prescription drug plans in your particular geographic area by going to the Medicare website at https://www.medicare.gov/part-d/coverage/part-d-coverage.html and clicking on "Find health & drug plans" to enter your zip code.

You can reassess your Part D coverage every year during an annual open-enrollment period from October 15 to December 7. You can look at plan options, your medication needs, and your costs and select the plan each year that is best for you. If your drugs have changed or if your plan has changed, your out-of-pocket expenses could be very different than they were the year before, even if your premiums remain pretty much the same.

Chapter 13

GETTING YOUR
LEGAL HOUSE IN ORDER

Most of my clients are not comfortable losing 30, 40, or 50 percent of their money in one year. Therefore, I have created systems that are designed to help my clients maximize their returns, minimize volatility, and find ways to generate inflation-adjusted income for life.

But what if you lost 30, 40, or 50 percent of your estate because you didn't have proper estate documents? Estate planning requires legal advice that will make sure your estate is going to be distributed the way you would like. If done properly, estate planning can greatly reduce the taxes required upon your death. My clients look to me to coach their financial lives. I don't give legal advice, but I do refer clients to two local estate planning attorneys who are very good at what they do: Richard Tizzano and John Kenney.

I've interviewed both Richard and John for this book and included their interviews below. I hope you might glean a little something from each of them. I have listed their contact information at the end of each interview as a resource for you and especially for those folks who reside right here in Kitsap County.

The purpose of each interview was to determine the basic estate documents everyone should have. In some cases, we also discussed a few of the lesser known and advanced estate planning concepts briefly.

A WORD OF CAUTION! Estate planning and the laws around this subject are unique to the state in which you live. Because most of the people I serve are here in Washington State, I focused on the issues in Washington State. Obviously if you are reading this outside of Washington State, you should consult with an expert estate planning attorney in your area.

INTERVIEW WITH RICHARD TIZZANO

JASON: Richard, I was hoping you could start out with helping me understand what exactly is estate planning?

RICHARD: I like to say estate planning is different from financial planning; financial planning folks help you grow your money, and good estate planning can help you distribute your money in a most effective manner to the people and the charities you want to see blessed, and perhaps even give you a strategy for how to do that while you're alive, as well as after you've died.

JASON: What are some of the essential documents everybody should have when developing an estate plan?

RICHARD: Everyone should have a power of attorney for financial matters, a power of attorney for medical matters, a living will, which in Washington is called a directive to physicians, and a will. Then it might be appropriate for some folks to have a living trust, special needs trust, or life insurance trust, or some other more advanced-type estate planning documents.

JASON: I would like to get some clarification on what each one of these documents is and what its purpose is. So what exactly is the power of attorney for financial matters, and why does somebody need it?

RICHARD: You would be authorizing someone to assist you with financial matters. It does not limit or take away your ability to control and manage your own finances, but it allows someone else to participate. That can be done in a few different ways. You can have someone not be appointed until some event happens where you become incapacitated, and in that scenario, the authority would be springing into effect when you were deemed to be incapacitated, either you had some accident or at some point your dementia is at a level where the doctor is willing to say, "No, you're not able to manage your own affairs."

Or it can be effective immediately when you sign the document. I recommend people consider that first, because it makes it much easier for a person to receive help from the person he or she trusts. The document doesn't have to be given out immediately when the person signs it, but the person has it, and if something unforeseen happens, then the person named, who is aware he or she has been named, can come and get the document and act on the person's behalf.

The more typical scenario is where someone begins to become more frail or have a bad day or whatever and needs somebody to take care of something, and if the document is effective immediately when it was signed, the person needing help can just give the other person the document and ask him or her to go take care of the matter with the financial institution. The same goes with a power of attorney for medical. The person can go talk to the doctor or access records immediately. The person does not have to have a determination of incapacity just to effectuate the document.

JASON: Who do people usually list as their power of attorney?

RICHARD: They usually list their spouses first and then a child they may trust or a child who may have a specific ability as an accountant or physician or something, and then after that, it is friends or neighbors.

JASON: Do you have a specific example of a time when somebody had a power of attorney and it really helped him, or a time when somebody probably should have had a power of attorney, and it really handicapped him because he didn't have that type of document?

RICHARD: I can combine it into one story that will make you aware of the shortcomings of a power of attorney. A son came in whose his dad was failing. He felt like his dad really needed to be in a nursing home, but his dad didn't want to go. The son had power of attorney for his father, and said as much to his dad, thinking he could force his dad to go. His dad got angry and said, "Well, I'm revoking the power of attorney."

That is one of the aspects of a power of attorney; unless it is agreed to by all parties or opposed by the court, it's revocable at any time.

I tell people when they sign it, if the agent or attorney-in-fact doesn't do what you want him to do, you can always fire him. So the dad fired the son, and the son felt powerless and said, "Well, I'd like to get a guardianship of my dad."

I explained to him that even if he were named as the guardian for his dad, he wouldn't have the authority to force his dad to do what he doesn't want to do. He would, however, have the authority to control his father's checkbook and his finances, and the court action would cut off his father's ability to access his own finances.

In Washington, we have what's called "the right to rot," which gives his dad the ability to decide what kind of care he wants or doesn't want. Even if the court deems him to be incompetent, you can't impose a level of care on him that he doesn't want unless there is an imminent danger to him or others, and that is a pretty high standard. If he doesn't want to take his medication, doesn't want to go to the nursing home, and wants to sit in front of the TV and eat bonbons and drink beer, he can do whatever he wants to do.

Having to have guardianship is a consequence of not having a power of attorney, but having a guardianship does not necessarily solve all the problems that come along with it. So, if someone does not have a power of attorney, whether it is for medical or healthcare, and he or she gets to the place where he is not able to care for himself, a guardianship has to be appointed.

I get people who come in occasionally and say, "Well I noticed my neighbor isn't taking the garbage out, and the mail is piling up in the mailbox. I went and visited him, and he seemed to be okay, but something's just not right." So we try to find out where the person's kids are or who the person is connected to. Sometimes there's nobody around, and it's either the neighbor, or the sister-in-law in Arizona trying to figure out how she's going to manage as the guardian for her sister-in-law up here who has to find someone locally who can assist her in that guardianship.

If you are one of those people now in need, but you don't have any powers of attorney because there was really nobody who was close enough to you that you wanted to select, or you just didn't know you needed a power of attorney, and then you get to the place where you need help, without those simple documents, it is going to require a guardianship before the court. The court will have to make a determination whether you are or you're not competent to manage your own affairs. If you're not, then the court will choose the most logical person who can step in and do that on your behalf, and if there is no obvious person like a relative or close friend, then it will assign a professional guardian who would have to step in at that point and fill that role.

JASON: So, if you don't take it upon yourself to have these documents in good order before they are needed, then the court has to get involved in determining who it thinks would be the best person for filling that role? Most people probably don't want the court making that decision for them I would imagine.

RICHARD: Well, I would agree, most people don't, but it's sad that a lot of people don't have an option. They don't go to church, or there's nobody in the church they've gotten close to, or all the people they have been close friends with have died. They have other peers, but they were never really close to those people, and their kids are far away, or they don't have kids, so they don't really have an option. It's not just a matter of realizing that, "Gee, I should name somebody," and having the inertia to get it done. Sometimes it's beyond that. I've had people come in and they want to get it done, but when I ask the question, "Who would you name?" I get a blank stare. They just realize there is nobody in their lives they can trust to do that, and they think that maybe I have an accountant I could trust for the financial part, so sometimes it gets really difficult.

JASON: So the medical power of attorney is different from the financial. The financial is going to give that person the ability to act on his or her behalf on financial matters, but what does the medical power of attorney give someone? How much authority, if somebody has a medical power of attorney, does that person have? Does the person just have the ability to access doctor's records or does he or she have the ability to make medical decisions for people?

RICHARD: Well again, you're authorizing someone to act on your behalf, but it does not take away your ability to act on your own behalf. I used to have a medical power of attorney that would be effective when you became incompetent, but again, I think this is a situation where the document is most effective if it's effective immediately because with the new health privacy act, the doctors are reluctant even to give medical information to your spouse.

If you have a power of attorney for healthcare that is effective immediately and your spouse wants to call the doctor, or if you're named on there for your parent and you want to call the doctor, you can fax it over to the doctor and say it's effective immediately. The doctor can then say, "Yeah, I did see your mom last week and this is what happened," or "These are the drugs I prescribed," or "This is the problem." If you decide, "Well, mom, you need a second opinion," you can call the office, arrange to have the records sent, and if the power of attorney is effective immediately, that allows you to do that, but again, if your mom says, "No, I don't want you to meddle; I'm going to revoke the power of attorney," she could always do that because she still maintains that control.

JASON: What is the living will and why is that important?

RICHARD: The living will or directive to physicians is important because it is addressing a situation where you are no longer able to tell the medical community what kind of care you want, so either your dementia has gotten so bad you can't communicate, or you're highly medicated, you have a head injury, you have some kind of terminal illness, death is imminent, or you can't communicate, so the person you've named in your power of attorney for your healthcare has the authority to assert this other document, this directive to physicians or this living will, on your behalf to address the kind of care you would want now that you're at the end of your life.

So you can't tell them at that point, "Because I'm dying and I can't eat, I do not want a feeding tube," but this document addresses those issues. Your status as attorney-in-fact, under the power of attorney, asserts that power and can tell the doctor that when the person was competent he said if death were imminent, he didn't want a feeding tube, he did not want hydration, or he did not want pain medication. It says here if his heart stops under these circumstances, he does not want CPR. It can address all those end-of-life issues.

I explain to people we can put whatever they want in there. One client said, "Well, I want you to put down that when I die, I'm buried with a cell phone, a candy bar, and a flashlight." I said we can do that, and then she laughed and said she was only kidding, but I have some people who are Jehovah's Witnesses, so they can't take a blood transfusion, and they want that in the directive to the physicians. They do not want that kind of care. My partner had a female client who said if they pass a piece of Hawaiian pizza under her nose three times and there's no reaction, then they can go ahead and disconnect her.

JASON: What about a will? Why is a will important, who should have one, and what does a will do?

RICHARD: A will directs whom you want to manage your estate after your death, so it allows for the appointment of an executor. The executor has some duties by law to open the probate, to advertise your death to the creditors, to consolidate or marshal all the aspects, to pay any taxes if there are any, and to assess and pay any creditors' claims if they're valid, and then to distribute what's remaining to all of the named beneficiaries as you have described in your will.

The misconception a lot of people have is now that they have a will, their kids can avoid probate, but a will doesn't avoid probate.

The will is the document that is used in the probate process to appoint the people you want appointed and to direct how you want things distributed.

JASON: I know when meeting with your clients that probate is a concern for them. What exactly is probate? I know it is a public process. What can you tell us about it, and why might people be hesitant to go through probate? How much time does it take?

RICHARD: I'm licensed in California and in the state of Washington and the process is pretty different in both states in the sense that California is much more detailed, much more involved, and the court is much more a part of the process, and therefore, I would say it is approximately ten times more expensive to do a probate in the state of California than in the state of Washington. So in California, people have a real sense of urgency to avoid the probate process, and that is where the living trust idea is effective. In Washington, the process is not nearly as onerous, and it is not nearly as expensive.

JASON: Is it likely to change or is it likely to stay as simple and as clean as it is now?

RICHARD: I don't see any move in the legislature toward change. There is legislation coming along in the area of protecting vulnerable adults, but nothing that I can see impacting probate. I think the public is satisfied for the most part with that probate process.

JASON: So, in the state of Washington, because it is a simpler, cleaner process, and less expensive maybe than California, how long would you say the average probate takes to have somebody's estate distributed according to the will?

RICHARD: An estate that does not include real estate would probably on average take nine months. There is a statutory requirement that the probate has to be open at least four months to allow for creditors' claims. The person dies and it takes a few weeks to get to the attorney, and then it takes a couple of weeks to get it open with the court. Then once the executor is appointed and the notice to creditors is published in the paper, the four-month period starts, so by the end of the four months, you are already six months down the line.

Once the creditors' claim period is over, then the executor is free to distribute assets because no creditor claims can be accepted after that period of time. The executor is free to distribute it without worrying that some creditor is going to show up and want to be paid. Then the receipts from the beneficiaries are filed and probate can be closed.

JASON: One of the concerns I have heard people express is that probate is a public process. Why would that be a concern to people?

RICHARD: Well, I got a book from a friend one Christmas called *Wills of the Rich and Famous*. All this author had done was get copies of famous people's wills from the court files by going around to the different jurisdictions where these famous people had died and where their wills were probated. He put them all together and made a book out of it. I think Jackie Kennedy was in there, John Kennedy, Frank Sinatra, and a couple of baseball players, so it was interesting.

A lot of it was just legalese, but I kind of cut to the dicey parts about whom they were leaving stuff to and how they were trying to avoid taxes or whatever. Some people are very private, and they are uncomfortable with the idea that anybody, even the black sheep of the family whom they don't want to know their business, can just go down to the courthouse and ask for the file and be allowed to look at it and see who got what. There's an inventory that's usually filed with the court so people can see everything you had and who got it.

JASON: Does a living trust come into play for people who don't want a nine-month process with probate or want a more private closing of their affairs?

RICHARD: Yes.

JASON: So, before we talk about the living trust, I just want to recap; for the bare minimum that everyone should have, the four documents are: the power of attorney for financial matters, the power of attorney for medical matters, a living will, and a will. Is that correct?

RICHARD: Yes.

JASON: So tell us a little bit more about living trusts. Who would want a living trust, and why might he or she want the living trust?

RICHARD: Okay. Let me touch on the issue of the probate with real property because sometimes, in the market we have now, real property is going to be a problem.

JASON: What do you mean by real property?

RICHARD: Houses or anything that is connected with land. Some people might own their house or a rental or a resort place or a condo. That is an asset that may be hard to distribute if you have three kids and want to divide your estate equally between them.

If you have $300,000 in the bank, each kid gets $100,000 and you're done. If there is the house mom and dad have lived in for years, and then there's the little rental they have up the street, and $75,000 in the bank, it is more problematic in distributing that to the three kids. Decisions have to be made. Are the kids going to co-own the house, or put the house up for sale? When it comes to cleaning up the house, who is going to do it? All of those things take a lot of time to process through, so what may not seem like a quick nine months is a pretty quick time to get that all taken care of when it's just cash in the estate, but when you have these other assets in the estate, that time can really drag on.

I have seen where you have a couple of the kids think they can't sell the place, and they want to keep it and visit it every summer, so they may hang onto it for a year or two, but then they realize how expensive it is and how impractical it is, and finally after a couple of years, they've come to the conclusion that they need to sell it. Sometimes the estate stays open while that happens; sometimes they transfer it so just the siblings all own that property jointly.

Real property is often a fly in the ointment as far as trying to distribute it efficiently or to close a probate.

Now that kind of issue is often the same, even if the assets are passing through a living trust versus a probate. So the way it works with a living trust is a twin of you is created; so it's not a separate entity in that it has a separate tax ID number, but it's a separate entity exactly like yourself. It has your own Social Security number. So this entity, which is not John Smith, but is the John Smith Trust, is created. It has John Smith's Social Security number, and John Smith is the trustee of it, and all the assets are controlled by John Smith Trustee. This legal fiction of sorts exists, and when John Smith the person dies, the John Smith Trust continues and then Mary Smith, who's named as the successor trustee, steps into John's shoes, and then Mary has the authority, as trustee, the same authority that John had to administer those assets, to manage them, to sell them if need be.

The trust directs that, when John dies, the three kids get what they're going to get, and then Mary has the authority to do whatever needs to be done to see that happens, pay the creditors if there are any, pay off other bills there may be, and consolidate the assets and distribute them to the beneficiaries. Mary can do all of that without court intervention because the trust owns the assets or controls the assets because they were titled in John Smith's name as trustee.

Usually, when a trust is created, a will is also created, and that will is called a pour-over will. It's a pour-over will by definition because the beneficiary of a pour-over will is the trust, so any particular asset that may show up that for some reason was not titled in John Smith's name may have to be probated, and then it pours over to the trust and is distributed according to the terms of the trust.

For example: John buys a winning lotto ticket, and then when he realizes it's the winning lotto ticket and he is going to get a million dollars a year for the next twenty years, he's so excited he dies of a heart attack. So John owns this asset; it's his, but it's not in his trust. There is no provision for the lotto people to pay the trust. It's John's ticket, and he went down to claim it just before he died, but again it's not in his trust, so what happens to that string of payments? Well, it has to go through probate.

The ticket is something John owned. He did not own it as trustee in his trust. He owned it individually, so there would be a probate of that particular asset and the beneficiary in the will is going to be the trust, so that pours into the trust, and then the new trustee in the trust would include the lottery winnings as the assets of the trust to be distributed with the other assets.

JASON: Okay. So if you have a living trust, then a pour-over will is an additional document you would have to make sure anything not titled will end up in the trust and be distributed the way you want. I have heard you should consider a trust in Washington State if you own real property outside of the state. Why might that be?

RICHARD: That is one of the questions I ask folks when they want some advice on getting a trust. I ask them, "Do you want to avoid probate?" Some people have had a good experience with probate, and they don't care, but for some people, for whatever reason, the probate has been a nightmare and they will say, "I absolutely don't want my kids to have to go through probate."

I ask them, "Do you have a taxable estate?" and we can talk about that in a minute, and "Do you own property in states other than Washington State?" Having a trust allows you to avoid probate, not only in Washington, but you can avoid probate in any other state in which you own real property. Otherwise, there has to be a probate.

It's called an ancillary probate when it's not for a state where you are a resident. If you own property in that state, a probate needs to be done to transfer that property to wherever you want to transfer it, if it's not held in your trust. So when I have clients who own property in a few states, I tell them, "It's a no-brainer; you need to have a trust."

JASON: What is the proper term when somebody is a trustee who takes over?

RICHARD: Successor trustee.

JASON: Is it a good idea to have more than one executor or more than one successor trustee, or can that cause problems?

RICHARD: It depends on whether the person you named is able to do it by him or herself, and whether he or she will do a good job or not. I have had some people who have kids who have fought like cats and dogs their whole lives, but they think, "When I die, it will bring my kids together. If I name them as co-trustees, they will be able to start this new relationship."

That's a mistake. You need to name someone you trust and who can at least balance a checkbook. The person must like to pay attention to detail and appear to be responsible in the financial area. The person is not a procrastinator. That is the kind of person you would want to be your trustee, and I have seen it where co-trustees have worked very well. It is a little more cumbersome because there are a number of situations where both people have to sign off on certain activities, and it may take a little more time or effort to get a few basic things done, but I think if the people get along, it can be helpful to have co-trustees. But if they don't get along, then there will be hell to pay.

JASON: Just a moment ago you mentioned a taxable estate. Would you speak to that for a moment?

RICHARD: Sure. There is a federal estate tax and a Washington State estate tax. That tax amount has changed over the course of time at both the state dollar amount and the federal dollar amount.

When a person dies, if he or she has a surviving spouse, the assets are able to pass to the surviving spouse without any state or federal estate tax because there is an unlimited marital deduction. Bill Gates could die and his surviving spouse would have no estate tax to pay, but when an individual dies or the surviving spouse dies, then all of their assets are added together.

That would include life insurance, retirement accounts, real property, toys, vehicles, boats, investment accounts, and timeshares.

Everything you own is added up together, and if that total exceeds the amount that is allowed for you to pass on without imposing the estate tax, then it passes the state tax-free. But if it exceeds that number, then your estate is subject to paying that tax and the estate pays the tax, not the beneficiaries.

You can do a few things to reduce having to pay that tax, and they basically come down to reducing the size of your estate or the total value of your estate when you die. You could take advantage of the annual gift tax exemption. For 2018 it is $15,000. It is ratcheted for inflation, so it may rise as time goes on, but it allows you to give money away to individuals at $15,000 a year to as many individuals as you wish.

If you have a lot of family, friends, and relatives, you could give each of those people $15,000. You could give your attorney $15,000, and your investment adviser $15,000, whoever you want. You can whittle away at your estate pretty quickly using the annual exclusion, and there is the unlimited marital exemption we talked about, so money could go to your spouse, but that would ultimately be subjected to tax.

You could give money to charity. If you give it to charity while you're alive, you get an income tax reduction. If you wait until you die, any money you give to charity at that point is deducted to your taxable estate and would go to charity, so you wouldn't have to pay any estate task on that amount, but your estate does not get an income tax deduction for the contribution to charity at your death.

JASON: Let me just run a quick example by you. Right now, today, and I know this is a moving target, so these numbers are going to change, but let's say there is a husband and wife. The husband dies. He ends up leaving everything to the wife, and now the wife has an estate of $15 million and she dies. So the couple had a total estate of $15 million. Are they looking at an estate tax with a $15 million estate? And if so, what would be the tax rate at the federal government approximately, and what would the state estate tax be? And I know this is probably some complex tax planning, but I'm just trying to get an idea for our readers what the consequences could be for people.

RICHARD: Okay. Well, for 2018 the Washington State estate tax is on any assets above $2.193 million per person, and the federal estate tax is on assets above $11.18 million. Both of those exemptions are subject to the marital deduction. If you die, and you have just a simple "I love you will" and you want to pass everything to your spouse, that passes to the surviving spouse and is not subject to that tax, so taxes do not have to be paid after the death of the first spouse.

JASON: So when the husband dies, the wife gets all $15 million, and she does not owe any estate tax at that point?

RICHARD: Correct. However, as we walk down this scenario, we will see that this simplicity on the first to die has a cost.

JASON: Ok, so now she dies. She has $15 million. How much would her estate tax be after the $11.18 million federal limit? Do you know what the current federal estate tax is?

RICHARD: It is 40 percent above the $11.18 million.

JASON: And the Washington State estate tax for amounts above the $2.193 million, any idea what that is?

RICHARD: The Washington estate tax is a graduated tax that starts at 10 percent and goes to 20 percent. So the entire amount over $2.193 million, or $12.807 million, would be subject to the Washington estate tax. That would be about $2.2514 million for the Washington estate tax and $627,440 for the Federal estate tax for a total of $2.8788 million! That doesn't even include any income tax that would have to be paid to cash out any qualified plans like IRAs or annuities.

Now, if the first spouse had made a 'portability' election, which we will discuss in a bit, they could have eliminated the Federal tax, but the Washington tax is still payable.

JASON: So worst case scenario for a higher net worth person is that almost 50 percent of his or her estate could be lost to taxes above those exclusion amounts without some proper planning.

RICHARD: Correct. So if this couple had a properly written living trust or will, they could have provided for a credit trust to hold $2 million of the $7.5 million that belonged to husband when he died. That would have set aside that amount under the Washington exemption of the husband, and the wife would have gotten all the income from that, and then the additional $5.5 million that belonged to the husband—we will just assume it was his community property—that could be held in a qualified terminal interest property trust or a QTIP trust, which the Washington estate tax would not have to be paid on until the wife died.

In our scenario, this simple step would have saved $400,000 in Washington estate tax alone!

JASON: So if someone has an estate that is worth $5-$10 million+, they should consult with an estate planner one-on-one because their needs will be more specific.

Or if they are around fifty years old and have an estate that is about $2.5 million dollars now, they should also meet with an estate planner because they should assume that their money, if it is earning 8 percent, over the next thirty years will double every nine years. This will quickly put them above the state and federal exclusions, so some planning may need to happen so they don't run into any estate tax problems in the future.

RICHARD: An interesting part of that $11.180 million, though, is if one spouse doesn't use it all, what was not used can shift over to the surviving spouse, if the surviving spouse is working with qualified professionals who file a Federal 'portability' election upon the first to die. So if the first spouse dies and the couple had an estate of $18 million, and the first spouse sheltered $94 million in their trust, and the surviving spouse's assets grew to $16 million dollars, then the estate of the second spouse to die would have their own $11.180 million plus the 2.18 million, which the first spouse didn't use to shelter their assets from Federal taxes.

Unfortunately, there is no 'portability' election for the Washington estate tax, so the only way to effectivey use both Washington estate tax credits is proper planning while both spouses are still alive.

JASON: Could you maybe touch briefly on when an irrevocable life insurance trust or a special needs trust might be needed, and who should be setting those up?

RICHARD: If you have a loved one who has a special need such as a disabled child, or maybe you want to remember your parent in your documents, whether it's your will or your trust, you can name that person as a beneficiary, but you must state that the share the person gets should be held in a special needs trust for the person's benefit.

So you would name somebody who would be the trustee of that trust for his or her benefit, and by doing it that way, rather than giving the person the money outright, you allow for a pool of money to be reserved to assist that person without interfering with the state or federal aid he or she may be getting.

So if you have a parent who is on Medicaid in a nursing home and you left him or her $50,000, he or she is going to be suddenly ineligible for Medicaid. If you left it to your parent in a special needs trust, then the trustee could use that money to provide extra care for your parent or get him or her an electric wheelchair or a van or something that Medicaid isn't going to pay for and the pool of money doesn't disqualify your parent from being eligible to continue to receive that Medicaid. The same would be true for a child who might be receiving assistance.

JASON: I see this concern come up a lot with parents of special needs children. They are worried their children will be cut off from some of these resources because of a lump-sum inheritance so a special needs trust would take care of that. What about the irrevocable life insurance trust? Who needs it, when does it come into play, and why do people look at those?

RICHARD: Most of the time as people age, they decide they don't need life insurance anymore. They don't have little kids at home,

and they have a different pool of money. But an irrevocable life insurance trust might be helpful, especially a second-to-die policy which moves funds out of your estate into this trust.

If it is an irrevocable life insurance trust, it is not part of your estate when you die for estate tax purposes. You could cover possible taxes that may have to be paid at your death, pay off mortgages, or other things you think need to be taken care of when you die. You might be concerned about whether or not there's going to be liquid cash available in your estate to cover those kinds of things.

JASON: This would be especially important for people who have a lot of their wealth tied up in real estate since the federal government requires that the inheritance tax/estate tax be paid within a certain period of time, and cashing in the real property could take too long for you to pay the taxes on time. This creates a pool of money the beneficiaries could use for that.

RICHARD: It could be used to cover that or even a family business that has been inherited so it wouldn't have to be sold. It is a good way to generate the cash to pay possible taxes.

JASON: Some people put off getting even their basic estate planning documents created because they hear that attorneys charge $200, $300, or $400 per hour. What is a fair amount they should probably expect to pay to get those estate documents completed?

RICHARD: Well, it certainly depends on where your local attorney lives or practices, and it is a function of the time it takes the attorney to create the documents. But when you look at it in relation to some of the advertisements you hear that say, "Send in $29 and you can get this program that will give you a will for your estate and powers of attorney and you need to do it now," there really is a sense that what people are doing is basic, but there are also just some very key questions that need to be addressed that make it complicated, where it is just worth having assistance from that person who has been down the trail before you and can guide you along the way.

For instance, a simple will is pretty basic. You're going to name your executor and whom you want to get your assets, but as I referred to earlier, let's say you want to leave something to your mom or you have a disabled child; just being able to have that special needs trust provision in your document is going to make sure that what you want accomplished gets accomplished.

I have people who are older, and it's the same kind of thing with them. People have been married for years so they want to name each other. They don't want to name the kids, even if it means preserving some assets, so they can have a special needs provision for their spouse that says when I die, my half of the community property is held for the benefit of my spouse in a special needs trust. If the person dies and then the surviving spouse ends up going into a nursing home, that's half the estate that's salvaged from or not available for many key purposes.

JASON: I tell my clients there is a time to try to cut costs, and there's a time to make sure you're doing things right. The concern I have is if you do them wrong, you could end up costing yourself a lot more money in the long run, so you don't want to be pennywise and a pound foolish as the saying goes. But what would the possible range be for the basic package?

RICHARD: Sure, I was just kind of confirming that there is some value there. I think for a single person to get all of the documents we talked about—the powers of attorney, the directive to physicians, and the basic will—it will cost a minimum of about $400-$500. It will take a minimum of two meetings with your attorney plus the creation of the actual documents, which easily brings the total time for the attorney to a minimum of four hours.

If we are talking about a couple, you might expect to pay $750-$1500 to get all those documents done for both people.

If you're talking about a trust, you have the documentation on the trust, and then I generally recommend the attorney also handle transferring all the assets into the trust so it is done properly. If you don't transfer the assets to your trust properly, then you end up having to go through the whole probate as if you hadn't created a trust. There is a lot more work in the trust preparation, but for a single person, I think you would expect to pay $1,000-$1,500 minimum, and probably $2,000 or so for a couple.

JASON: So for a range of costs, we are talking anywhere from $400-$5,000 depending on how complex the estate is.

RICHARD: Sure. I think that is very well put.

JASON: Thank you, Richard. I appreciate your time here.

Sherrard, McGonagle, Tizzano
Attorneys at Law, Est. 1954
Richard C. Tizzano, PS
19717 Front Street
PO Box 400
Poulsbo, WA 98370
(360) 697-7132
richardt@legalpeaceofmind.com

INTERVIEW WITH JOHN KENNEY

JASON: John, what exactly is estate planning, why is it important, and what are some of the essential documents that everybody should have?

JOHN: Estate planning is a method whereby an individual, couple, or family can create a plan or a structure in order to prepare for an eventual or potential incapacity and inevitable death. The idea and the notion behind estate planning is that you want to make sure **you** decide what happens with yourself, your property, and/or your minor children, rather than having the State decide or the State laws decide. Good estate planning would be something that carries out your plans and wishes, as well as minimizes every tax or cost possible so your family is not unnecessarily burdened with those kinds of taxes and costs. A number of components make up proper estate planning.

JASON: One of the consequences of not having estate documents is you don't get to decide how your estate is going to be distributed; what happens then? You mentioned the State has a plan?

JOHN: Yes, the State has laws that decide how an individual's property will be divided and distributed if that person or married couple does not have an estate plan. For example, I recently had a prospective client whose husband had died without a will. So dad died, mom is still alive, and dad has adult children from a prior relationship. The title of the real estate the husband and wife owned did not clearly state whether the wife had a "right of survivorship." dad's adult children could potentially lodge a claim against the home that the husband thought was going to his wife when he died because he did not have a will. These examples come up all the time, but the State has a plan, and it is not always what the person, couple, or family desires.

JASON: Okay, I know there are different levels of estate planning depending on people's needs, but what are the basic documents that everyone should have regardless of the level of wealth he or she has?

JOHN: Sure. I will go through them and then I will circle back and explain why. At minimum, everyone should have a will and a financial power of attorney, also called a durable power of attorney. You should also have a healthcare power of attorney and a living will. Another document you'll need is a HIPAA authorization, which is now required by the Health Insurance Portability and Accountability Act.

A will basically does two primary things for a person: it divides your property according to your wishes, and if you have minor children, it will name guardians for those children. Without it, the State or courts will decide how your property is distributed and who will take care of your minor children if you, or your spouse, pass away.

The financial power of attorney, which is often called a durable power of attorney, gives someone else the power to make decisions for you if you become incapacitated and are unable to manage your own financial or legal affairs because of a legal condition, a health condition, or some other thing that is affecting your capacity to make decisions.

The document will assign an agent or attorney-in-fact to make those decisions for the individual who is incapacitated. Without it, the State will decide how your legal and financial affairs are going to be managed, and the State will appoint someone to do that for you.

Some people say, "Well, I don't care; let the State decide," but the process of letting the State decide can be very expensive for anyone you've left behind. Whereas, creating a will and/or durable power of attorney would allow your family to avoid that unnecessary expense and avoid allowing the state to take the control out of your hands.

JASON: Whom do people typically appoint as their financial power of attorney or their durable power of attorney?

JOHN: If it is a married couple and the other spouse is capable, the healthy spouse is usually appointed. I say healthy spouse because one will be unhealthy or incapacitated if the durable power of attorney has to come into play. Oftentimes, we will also have clients name a secondary person because it is possible that the spouse could either die or become incapacitated also. Clients will often appoint adult children if they have adult children who are responsible and they trust.

It is important that the individual be trustworthy and capable of managing someone's legal and financial affairs. If clients do not have adult children or spouses whom they trust or who are capable, they will name a trusted friend, and ultimately, if they do not have any friends who are capable or who they trust, they could name a professional such as a CPA, attorney, or financial adviser whom they trust or have trusted in their lives.

JASON: Why do they call it either financial or durable power of attorney?

JOHN: People use powers of attorney at various times throughout their lives. If you are buying a car, the dealer will actually give you what is called a limited power of attorney so the dealer can file your title and registration for you when you purchase that car. Anyone who has bought a car has probably signed one of these things. Limited purpose powers of attorney expire when the person's purpose is completed.

Often, you will give power of attorney to a spouse to accomplish certain tasks. Those are also limited and expire. If you become incapacitated, you don't want your power of attorney to expire, so a durable power of attorney will endure your incapacity and continue throughout it and not expire.

JASON: I want to back up just a minute. Will you speak for a minute about what probate is and how it works with a will?

JOHN: Absolutely. Basically there are four primary purposes of probate. Number one is, if an individual has a will, to take that will and read it, and ultimately, distribute the property or the assets to the individuals whom the will says to distribute them to and in the manner it states.

Secondarily, the purpose of probate is to notify any creditors of the death of this individual so the creditors can make a claim to get paid any money the deceased owed them. That is why you will often see in the newspapers long notices in the classified sections that will say "notice to creditors" of the probate of the deceased individual.

Third, as I mentioned before, is to appoint guardians for minor children if a person had minor children. The court actually appoints the guardian, but the will tells the court whom the deceased person wished to appoint.

The last purpose of a probate procedure is to notify all of the heirs or beneficiaries or people who want to claim to be an heir of the deceased. I often have clients who want to avoid probate so we will create a revocable living trust, which we can talk about later, because a revocable living trust avoids probate if created and implemented correctly.

I once had one client who told me he wanted to avoid probate because thirty years earlier he had an illegitimate child, and he wanted to avoid the notice that goes out in the paper so this individual wouldn't come to the probate process and try to make a claim against the net worth of his estate and emotionally upset his spouse.

In some states, probate can be very expensive. Thankfully, in Washington State it is not that expensive relative to other states, such as California. One thing many people do not know about or are unaware of, is that if they own property in multiple states, then a probate is necessary in every state where they own property. Property is not necessarily only real estate. It can be a timeshare that has a contract. It can be an investment account that you opened when you were in college in California. I had one client who died, and unbeknownst to his children, he had opened an investment account in LA while he was in college. It had grown to a substantial amount, but he had never transferred it to a local branch; the State of California made the family go through probate in California because California is one of those very expensive states and the state wanted its piece of the action.

Probate in Washington State, without an aggravating-factor, like out-of-state property, is not that expensive and not that problematic. By law, the court is required to take four months. That is the absolute minimum that a probate process can take because it is written in the law.

Typically, a standard-type probate will take six to nine months and sometimes a year. I did a probate that lasted five years because the individual who died had some creditors who were trying to come after that individual at the time of his death, so it took five years to resolve all of those creditors' claims. All the children of this individual stood waiting until the claims were resolved, and then the children were eventually paid their inheritance.

JASON: I heard probate is a public process, and that concerns some people. What is it that concerns people about it being a public process?

JOHN: It can concern people because they do not want people who claim to be their creditors to come after their spouse or their children, or to try and take their property. Also, as I mentioned, they may not want their potential heirs or probably more accurately, the people who claim to be heirs, to try and make a claim against the net worth of their estate.

More importantly, the probate files and court records are also available to the public. My partner and I have found Social Security numbers on numerous occasions when we were looking back at old probate records and court files.

These files contain the address of your real estate, the value of your real estate, and sometimes, they contain your Social Security numbers. They should not, but it happens. Anybody can check out files and find that information at the court clerk's counter, and in some counties in Washington where the records are all online, you could actually go online and find it. For people who have a desire to be private, it is not the best alternative because it is all public.

JASON: Jumping forward, what is healthcare power of attorney, why is it important, and who should have it?

JOHN: A healthcare power of attorney is similar to a regular power of attorney because it becomes effective if someone is incapacitated. An individual pre-approves or pre-appoints another individual, usually called a healthcare agent, who is healthy and able to make decisions, to make healthcare choices for that individual.

The healthcare choices can be as simple as the individual needing some surgery, but he or she is unconscious and not able to authorize it for him or herself, so the healthcare agent just goes ahead and authorizes the surgery. Then that individual wakes up, and he or she is fine.

It could also be as serious and grave as making the decision to remove life support, which is one of the specific powers usually appointed to the healthcare agent. I tell people to choose someone who has his or her head on his shoulders as far as managing finances and legal things for his financial power of attorney, but being a healthcare agent takes more than that.

Sometimes healthcare decisions have spiritual consequences. Sometimes they have heavy emotional consequences so the individual you are choosing to be your healthcare agent should have the ability to make these types of emotional and spiritual life-ending decisions.

Oftentimes, when an individual goes in for routine surgeries, the hospital will ask whether the person has a living will and healthcare power of attorney. The living will is yet another document that expresses an individual's desire if he or she is in a specific condition such as permanently brain dead, comatose, or other permanently ill-type conditions. There are a number of definitions, but those are the most common.

An individual makes a decision in advance about whether to be kept alive, meaning the body's brain is dead and not functioning, but medical providers are keeping the body's blood and lungs pumping indefinitely with machinery and respirators, or not. Would that individual prefer to have life support removed so he or she can just pass away? The medical agent or healthcare agent who is appointed in the healthcare power of attorney would make that decision with the family members in counsel with the doctors.

The reason these two documents are very important is, first, keeping somebody alive in the hospital without the proper legal authorization to remove life support can be very, very emotional on a family, and if no one is appointed to make that decision, sometimes the decision is never made.

The second consequence is financial. People fail to realize in the immediate situation, until a month or two later, the financial consequences. For instance, if a husband and wife did not have a lot of savings, did not have a living will and/or a healthcare power of attorney, could not make the decision, and let the individual kind of linger for a week or two, then the medical bills can be tens of thousands of dollars per day. I have had clients who said, "Yeah, mom had a living will, but we let her stay alive an extra three or four days to let the family fly in and gather, and it cost us an extra $100,000." People do not sometimes grasp the financial consequences you can leave your spouse with if, in fact, you do not have a document like this.

The final document, just to mention it briefly, that goes along with these other documents is the HIPAA authorization. Anybody who has ever been to a doctor in the last five or six years has signed something that has this acronym HIPAA on it.

In 2003, a federal law went into effect that says no individual is allowed to receive healthcare information about another individual without prior pre-authorization. This law made it illegal for medical providers to pass healthcare information to family members or healthcare agents without pre-authorization so the HIPAA authorization lists all these people and allows the medical providers to disclose that person's condition to them so they can make decisions regarding him or her. How can you make decisions if you can't be told what the condition is?

JASON: I have heard of people listing more than one executor on their wills to carry out their wishes. Is that a good idea?

JOHN: No. I try to counsel them out of it when they list joint executors or all three of their children as co-executors. I tell them of a horror story I once had with a client—an elderly woman who had emphysema. When she came to see me, she was probably going to die within a couple of years. She put down both of her children as co-executors. Up to that point, I had not had any personal experience with such cases, but the professors in law school always cautioned us about this kind of situation.

My client assured me that her children got along fine and were great friends. Within a couple of days of her death, both of her children called me and each one said the other was a drug addict and had been stealing from their mom for years and should not serve as an executor, but of course, the one speaking to me claimed to be capable and wanted to do it alone.

I was mom's attorney, so I withdrew from representing either of them. They then individually hired their own attorneys, and I was told by the attorneys that they spent about $10,000 sorting out who would be the personal representative. Sadly, that woman's estate was probably only worth about $60,000, so they drained about one-sixth of what they would have inherited just fighting over who would be personal representative. The personal representative only carries out a mechanical function. The person cannot give more money to him or herself. It was very unfortunate, but the lesson I learned is it can be problematic to have two executors because they always have to agree on everything. People are not always going to agree despite your thinking that they will do what is best.

JASON: When should people consider getting a revocable living trust and why would they want that in addition to having the basic documents?

JOHN: A lot of people think that having a revocable living trust is just for the wealthy, and to a certain extent, that is true. I do it for a lot of my higher net worth clients, but there is another reason that has nothing to do with your level of wealth: to avoid probate.

Probate is not a terrible process, but certain people want to avoid it entirely either because of the privacy issues, the time it takes, or the cost.

They may want to have the settlement of their estate be private, so with the revocable living trust, nothing is published in the newspaper. All the documents are kept with your attorney and family members. Nothing is given out, so the privacy factor is an important part of it.

Again, the probate process can take six to nine months on average, sometimes five years or longer. With a revocable trust, we can usually wrap up distributing property within thirty to forty-five days, unless there is real estate that has to be sold, which is dependent on the real estate market and not the laws.

The legal and attorney's fees for the distribution and wrapping up of the revocable living trust is usually going to be under $1,000, and probate, on average, in Kitsap County is about $3,000 to $5,000, so the cost savings that people can realize may be important to them.

On the other hand, a basic will is just that—very basic. It is not designed off-the-shelf to do a lot of things. Many of my clients have adult children who are married, and they don't just want their trustee or their executor to write a check to an adult child and say, "Here's your share." They want to protect that inheritance for their children from a child's potential divorce. When a parent sets up a trust and continues that trust for the benefit of a child or multiple children, that trust is in most cases exempt from divorce. It is also usually exempt from those children's creditors if they get into bad debt situations; it is exempt from creditors whom they may not know about; for instance, if they run somebody over in their car. It is also exempt from bankruptcy court, so if they file bankruptcy as a result of bad creditor problems, that trust is exempt.

Likewise, using a revocable living trust can provide protection if you are concerned about your spouse remarrying someone who might take the money from that spouse. The spouse can be provided for and receive money from the trust, and the trust can specify that the spouse cannot change it or give it away to the new spouse.

I had a situation where I worked on a case about two years ago. In fact, it is still ongoing. An individual who was a dentist and had $3-4 million had been married for thirty or more years when his wife passed away. He had four adult children at the time. He remarried a few years after his wife's death. The joke among the four adult children was that his new wife was a mail order bride because she had just shown up from Eastern Europe one day and they were married.

This second marriage lasted five or six years before he died. After his death, his second wife revealed that he had created a new will after they were married and the new will disinherited all four of his adult children and left all of his wealth to her and her children. They are now suing her on the only grounds they have—that he was incapacitated, because he had Alzheimer's, when he executed the second will.

The children do not have much of a chance to overturn the will. If their mom or dad had created a will or a revocable living trust that had protected the children's inheritance, then none of this would have been an issue. But of course, he fell in love with his new mail order bride and her children whom she imported from Eastern Europe, so his first wife's children were left with nothing when there was plenty to go around.

Finally, as I mentioned earlier, if you have property out-of-state including a bank or investment account or time-shares, you are usually required to go through probate in that other state. The costs can add up quickly if you take the cost of probate in Washington at $3,000-$5,000 and you add the other states' probate costs because you have an investment account in California, and a winter place down in Arizona—pretty soon you are looking at $15,000-$20,000 worth of legal fees. A lot of my clients who have winter places down in Southern California or Arizona set up a revocable trust to avoid probate in those states.

These are the high level, very general benefits of using a revocable living trust, and it definitely has some advantages over a basic will, but it is not for everyone. Someone with a very modest net worth, who does not care about avoiding probate and does not have property in multiple states, is probably just fine with a regular basic will.

JASON: I know some people put off getting these estate documents done because they are intimidated by lawyers and because they hear horror stories of costs ranging from $200-$500 per hour. Can you give our readers a range of what they could expect if a single person comes in, and he or she just wants the bare bones basic estate documents he or she should have? I know everybody's situation is going to be different, but just give us the big picture idea of what might be expected.

JOHN: I don't know if your audience geographically is all here in Kitsap County, but basically in Kitsap County, for any capable and competent estate planning attorney, a basic will package, and I say the word "package" because it includes all the powers of attorney we talked about, the living will, as well as a HIPAA authorization, should range anywhere from $600-$1,000 total when there are no complexities in the individual's situation. For a married couple, it would be double that amount. If you go over to King County, the fee is probably going to be $900-$1,500 for the same basic will package just because those attorneys are paid a lot more and the firms charge a lot more over there. These figures are just a general range and will vary for each situation.

JASON: So it could be as little as $600 and up to maybe $5,000 if somebody has a very complex trust or has several different trusts that need to be created?

JOHN: Yes, and if you go to a revocable living trust, you can generally add at least $1,000 onto that base fee of the basic will package. Oftentimes, as you mentioned, someone may have multiple trusts, which will cost more, and I haven't even mentioned life insurance trusts. A life insurance trust, commonly called an ILIT for the acronym representing irrevocable life insurance trust, is often used to help avoid estate taxes on life insurance policies.

Estate taxes are the taxes the State of Washington and the federal government can charge an individual after that person is dead. Often, people don't realize that the life insurance proceeds come into play under the estate tax as well. They may have $300,000 or $400,000 net worth, but also have $1-2 million in life insurance policies. It is very important when we talk to clients to evaluate what they have as far as their current net worth, as well as their life insurance because a life insurance trust can avoid all estate taxes for that life insurance policy.

JASON: What is going on with federal and state estate taxes?

JOHN: In 2018, the federal estate tax exemption, or credit as some call it, was changed and set at $11.18 million per person, adjusted annually for inflation. This is the amount of wealth, including life insurance proceeds, that each person can own before being taxed for estate tax purposes. If an estate plan is created correctly, then in 2018, a married couple could pass up to $22.36 million — free of federal estate taxes. This amount will go up each year. However, a certain amount of estate planning is required to insure that both spouses get their credit and that one credit is not lost on the first spouse's death. This is vital and can result in a lot of extra tax being owed if not done properly.

Now, a lot of my clients and a lot of individuals I work with here in Washington State were doing back flips and thinking, "Yay! I've got $5 million of net worth, and I don't have to pay estate tax on it." But a lot of the individuals in Washington don't realize that Washington has an estate tax and that Washington's estate tax credit does not match the federal credit. Washington's estate tax credit is only $2.193 million, so anything above $2.193 million is subject to Washington State's estate tax. Washington State's estate tax starts at 10 percent and tops out at 21 percent so for anything over the $2.193 million mark, you won't pay a federal tax if it's still under $11.18 million, but you could potentially pay a pretty high State of Washington tax. A married couple could avoid the Washington estate tax also but only with proper advance planning.

JASON: And what is the top rate for the federal estate tax if you have more than $11.18 million? Some of my clients may only have $5 million today, but they are only fifty years old, and if their money is compounding at 8 percent per year for the next thirty years—doubling every nine years—they could very easily end up with a sizeable estate.

JOHN: Right now, for the next two years, along with this $11.18 million credit, the top federal estate tax rate is 40 percent.

JASON: So potentially 61 percent of your taxable estate could go to paying estate taxes if you have a higher net worth between your federal estate taxes and taxes here in Washington State?

JOHN: Correct.

JASON: John, is there anything else you would like to add that you think would be relevant to the readers with respect to estate planning, basic documents, or other concerns people should be thinking about?

JOHN: As you mentioned earlier, a lot of people don't like talking to attorneys, but the good estate planning attorneys will try to make the experience proactive for the client. They want the client to participate in the process rather than just being told this is how they're going to do it. I have had clients complain that attorneys will just write something up, not explain it very well, and then just have them sign it.

Good attorneys will ask a lot of questions and usually charge a flat fee. The beauty of a flat fee is that clients don't have to fear the cost of the unknown fees. The unknown total of a project with an hourly charge of $150-$200 is scary. I charge a flat fee which means this is the analysis I have gone through, and for me to do the work we are proposing, it is going to be X dollars and no more. It provides a lot of certainty and can eliminate a lot of those fears.

Then the final thing I would mention is because we only have a two-year window with this current law, it is important now more than ever that individuals get in to see a capable and competent estate planning attorney so they can discuss their estate planning needs. Beyond 2012, we still don't know what will happen, so you have to have an estate plan that is designed and implemented to give you the maximum flexibility for whatever the estate tax laws will be.

The good estate planning attorneys will have documents and software that will create the maximum flexibility for your estate planning needs given the current laws. Be careful of attorneys who are one day a divorce attorney, the next a personal injury attorney, and then the next day your estate attorney. They are not always going to be on the cutting edge with all of their estate planning documents needed for designing a plan with the most flexibility.

JASON: That brings up a good question. You open up the phone book, you turn to "A" in the yellow pages, and there are ninety pages of attorneys listed. How do people know whether they are working with a good estate planning attorney? How can they help narrow that search, or what are some resources they could consider?

JOHN: Well, there are national organizations that give designations to estate planning attorneys. One of them is called American College of Trust and Estate Planning Counsel. I do not believe we have any ACTEPC estate planning attorneys here in Kitsap County; almost all of them are in Seattle. You should also choose one that has a narrower niche or only practices estate planning. For example, I practice business law, tax law, and estate planning. All three have to do with tax laws so my focus is pretty narrow and specific to those areas.

One thing that differentiates me from some of my colleagues here in Kitsap County is that I have what is called an LLM, which is a master's degree in tax law. That means I was sick enough to go back to law school for two more years beyond the regular three-year law degree to get more advanced training and education just in tax and estate planning, so look for that and any other designations the attorney may have. But the most important thing, especially in a community such as Kitsap County, is to ask whether the person's primary area of focus is estate planning. In Kitsap County, you see a lot of generalist attorneys who do a little bit of everything, which means they may not be very good at any one thing, and that can be dangerous and costly when it comes to estate planning.

JASON: All right. Thank you, sir.

Luce Kenney & Associates, PS
Attorneys at Law
John Kenney, LLM
17791 Fjord Dr NE Suite O
Poulsbo, WA 98370-8482
(360) 850-1049
john.kenney@lucekenneylaw.com
www.lucekenneylaw.com

SOUND RETIREMENT PLANNING

23,725 DAYS

I have had the good fortune to read the book *20,000 Days and Counting* by Robert Smith. I tend to read a lot of books, and this book has been my one of my favorites to read so far. The book is a short read. You can finish it in one sitting and, although, short it is full of great insights.

I recently met with a gentleman who was 65 years old and ready to retire. Did you know that if you live to age 65, then you have lived 23,725 days? The average life expectancy for a man age 65 is approximately age 82. If he is fortunate to live to life expectancy, then he has 6,205 days to live.

I asked this gentleman how he envisioned his retirement? How would he like to live out the final 6,205 days of his life? What is most important to him? As he sat back in his chair and looked up to the ceiling, he shared how he wanted to travel more, enjoy time with his wife, spend more time volunteering with his church, connecting with people who were important to him and be more involved with his grandchildren.

I never once heard him say, "Jason, I can't wait to spend my retirement years sitting in front of my computer managing my investments."

One of the things I've learned over the years and was reminded of when I read Robert Smith's book is that oftentimes the people who hire us do so, not because we can manage their investments better than they can, but because they don't want to waste their time on an activity that isn't their absolute best use of their most precious asset, their time.

A CELEBRATION FORMULA

"The purpose of life is not to be happy. It is to be useful, to be honorable, to be compassionate, to have it make some difference that you have lived and lived well." - Ralph Waldo Emerson

I feel so very blessed to serve amazing people. I have been given the gift of being able to work with people at a really wonderful time in their lives. People share with me their hopes, fears, disappointments, accomplishments, and dreams. The people we serve bring a lot of wisdom to our relationship. I feel obligated to share what I learn from these folks because it has made my life better. I hope it makes yours a little better also.

One of the disadvantages of working with retirees is that I am exposed to things like dementia, disease, and death more often than the average person my age. I've attended funerals, memorials, and celebrations of life. I recently had the opportunity to attend a celebration of life for a client, and I wanted to share what I learned.

Attending her service made me wonder if there was a formula you could construct for living a life worth celebrating. These are a few takeaways I garnered on what that celebration formula might look like. Below are some of the things I experienced directly from our relationship as well as things I learned about her from the folks who were also in attendance at her service.

- **Touch** — She had warm hands. Every time she came by my office the very first thing she would do was grab my hand with both of her hands, look me straight in the eyes, and ask, "How is your family?"

- **Ask questions & listen** — Many people at her service mentioned that she was a good friend and great listener. She asked lots of questions and made you feel special and important. She genuinely cared about what was happening in your life.

- **Give** — When she learned I enjoyed vegetable gardening, she sent me some heirloom tomato seeds from her garden for me to plant. Many told stories about how she would go out of her way to find out what people liked and then she would look for opportunities to be generous and give to others.

- **Care for people** — Her son told a story about how when they were kids on a family vacation his mom saw a man who looked homeless on a bicycle. She approached this dirty man, introduced herself and found out he was attempting to ride his bike around the world. She invited this stranger to their home, and he lived with them for two weeks before they helped him get to the next leg of his journey. He became a family friend, and they stayed in contact her entire life.

- **Have fun** — One neighbor stood up who was responsible for managing the private gravel road they lived on. He said at the top of the road there were always deep grooves in the gravel because she liked to get in her 1967 convertible Mustang, go to the top of the street, and spin the wheels a few times before she would drive down the street. She stood a little less than five feet tall but had a GREAT BIG personality.

- **Believe** — She believed in God and loved Jesus. What a comfort that was to her daughter as she stood before friends and family and said, "I know one day I'll see my mom again in heaven." In my opinion, her belief may have been one of the greatest gifts she ever gave.

The theme of the celebration was "love lives on." We were all given flowers to bring home and plant in our gardens. I hope sharing her story helps her legacy of love to live on. She had an impact on my life, and I hope this little snippet of her life may have an impact on yours.

FINAL THOUGHTS

I appreciate your taking the time to learn about some of the different ideas, concepts, and strategies I use to help my community and clients transition into and through retirement. I feel blessed to have some of the best clients in the world.

With 10,000 baby boomers retiring every day, and with all of the turmoil we are experiencing in our country and around the world, my hope is that you will be able to take some of these concepts and implement them into your own life so they will give you a greater sense of confidence and direction as you transition through this great time of your life.

Yogi Berra once said, "If you don't know where you are going, any road will take you there."

Conversely, when you have a written plan for achieving your retirement goals, you will be much more confident in where you are, where you are going, and how you will get there. I like what Peter Drucker once said, "The best way to predict the future is to create it."

Finally, I'd like to leave you with this one last thought. Many people spend their entire lives in the land of someday. Someday I'll travel, someday I'll retire, someday I'll spend more time with my loved ones, someday I'll write my memoir, and then all of a sudden, something happens. An accident or health event occurs and life changes, and "someday" becomes a lost dream that will never happen. I like the quote by James Oppenheim, "The foolish man seeks happiness in the distance; the wise man grows it under his feet."

May you grow happiness under your feet.

All the best,

Jason Parker

Jason Parker

Made in the USA
Columbia, SC
06 November 2018